Jump Shot: Kenny Sailors

JUMP SHOT

KENNY SAILORS

Basketball Innovator and Alaskan Outfitter

LEW FREEDMAN

WESTWINDS
PRESS®

Library of Congress Cataloging-in-Publication Data
TK

Designer: Rudy Ramos
Cover Photo: Kenny Sailors taking his signature shot, from the
1946 University of Wyoming Yearbook, courtesy of the American
Heritage Center, University of Wyoming.

Published by WestWinds Press®
An imprint of

GRAPHIC ARTS
BOOKS®

P.O. Box 56118
Portland, Oregon 97238-6118
503-254-5591
www.graphicartsbooks.com

Contents

ACKNOWLEDGMENTS

A special thanks to Tim Harkins, the head of the sports information office at the University of Wyoming for information and photographs provided.

Thanks also to Bill Schrage, Kenny Sailors's friend who maintains his website http://kennysailorsjumpshot.com.

Introduction

KENNY SAILORS IS A REMARKABLE MAN. He is a one-time college basketball star at the University of Wyoming where he introduced the use of the jump
shot as a potent weapon to the sport, and when the NCAA basketball tournament celebrated its seventy-fifth anniversary in 2013 Sailors was the oldest living most outstanding player.

At the time Sailors was ninety-two years old and could look back on a life
well lived, a life of grand achievement, and a life of contentment.

In 1943, when the Wyoming Cowboys won their only NCAA title, Sailors,
a 5-foot, 11-inch guard, was selected as the outstanding player of the tournament. After that he played during the first five years of the NBA's existence, a
role that had him shifting from team to team during the unstable years of the
fledgling league.

Always an outdoorsman, and really a cowboy at heart (not only a represen-
tative of a school that had that nickname applied to its sports teams), Sailors
and his wife, Marilynne, known as Bokie, operated dude ranches, camps for
boys, and hunting camps in Wyoming. Then, in 1965, they left behind their
childhood homes and set out for Alaska.

For the next thirty-five years Sailors worked as both a hunting guide and as
a high school basketball coach in remote Alaska communities. In 2000, Sailors
returned to his native Wyoming and he presently resides in Laramie, just a
short distance from the site of his collegiate athletic triumphs.

One day in 1988 when I was working as sports editor of the *Anchorage Daily
News*, Alaska's largest newspaper in Alaska's largest city, I received a letter from

a one-time professional basketball player whom I had heard of, but really knew little about. It was Kenny introducing himself to me.

At the time Sailors was living in the community of Angoon on Admiralty Island in Southeast Alaska and was coaching the girls' basketball team. It was uncharacteristic of the generally modest Sailors to pen such an introductory letter, but if his intent was to gain some attention for his small-school high school team, it worked.

The more I learned about this fellow living in a remote corner of the state, the more intrigued I became, and soon enough I was flying to Admiralty Island to meet him. I should note that I am usually averse to flying on small airplanes, but I convinced myself this one time it was worth it.

The first leg of the trip was an easy one, a jet ride to the state capital of Juneau. It was the second hop that had me concerned. Heavily sedated so I wouldn't get airsick, I was joined by *Daily News* photographer Bob Hallinen as the only passengers in a four-seat floatplane that carried us to a landing dock next to Admiralty Island.

Although the coming and going part to and from the island in the small craft was not the highlight of my life, spending time talking basketball with Kenny Sailors was one of them. He and his gracious wife, Marilynne, hosted us for several days. Seemingly we met everyone on the island, all of whom raved about what a great guy Sailors was, and I had a treat discussing basketball history.

Long after the magazine-length story appeared in the newspaper Kenny and I stayed in touch. To some extent, despite his success and his claim to fame as being the innovator of the jump shot, he was a forgotten basketball figure. Living in Wyoming and Alaska for decades had kept Sailors out of the mainstream.

My visit with the Sailorses at Admiralty Island was the beginning of a great friendship that has continued for more than twenty-five years. Kenny and I shared many experiences, from visits to his cabin home two hundred road miles from Anchorage, to taking brisk, few mile walks together on selected mornings. I should note that while Kenny is thirty years older than I am, he was still pretty much able to walk me into the ground with his pace during those little hikes through the woods. As far as I could tell the old athlete was still in darned good shape.

Kenny lived in bear country and I was always worried that a large, furry creature with sharp nails might sneak up on us, but Sailors did not seem particularly concerned that would occur and it never did.

We shared a fishing boat on the Gulkana River and family members joined me for horseback riding at Kenny's guiding headquarters in Gakona, Alaska.

We also shared time in Denver in 1990 when the NCAA men's basketball championships were conducted there and part of the week's theme was "A Salute to Rocky Mountain Basketball." Sailors was invited to speak at the kickoff dinner, which I also attended, and we sat in the stands together for the tournament semifinals at the Final Four.

It is difficult to imagine the sport of basketball without the jump shot. It is a fundamental part of every player's game. However, one does not have to borrow an H. G. Wells time machine to be reminded that in the 1940s just about everyone employed a set shot from outside and that it was taboo for a player's feet to leave the hardwood while taking a shot at the basket.

The two-hand set shot was the weapon of choice for the outside shooter. When a player was left unmolested by the defense some twenty-five feet away from the hoop he took a shot with both feet planted and both hands on the ball. Once in a while a comparative daredevil would take a one-hand push shot.

There have been various claimants to the honor of being the inventor of the jump shot. Hank Luisetti of Stanford was an acclaimed player who took a one-hand shot. However, despite those various believers and supporters of other players, many famous witnesses say that Sailors was indisputably the player who shot the jump shot that all basketball fans have come to know and that all future players have come to use.

Sailors himself never made the specific claim that he actually invented the jump shot, admitting that someone, somewhere may have taken one in a game here and there that he never knew about. Yet when Sailors was competing for Wyoming, no one else was taking jump shots in games. When Sailors was playing in the NBA, no one else was taking jump shots in games.

There is no doubt that Sailors was the first high-level practitioner of the shot and his reputation was solidified and assured for that historic accomplishment in November of 2012 when he was enshrined in the College Basketball Hall of Fame in Kansas City.

It was on that memorable day Sailors's innovation and achievement was formally ratified. The man that gave the world the jump shot was feted and honored with induction into a hall of fame that will forever celebrate his accomplishments and contributions to basketball.

For those of us, friends and relatives, who had long known Kenny's story, it was a heartfelt moment of pride and although he had waited many decades for such recognition, it was one that provided a glow for Sailors, too.

As the star of an indoor game, it might be seen as ironic that the rest of Sailors's life revolved around the outdoors. When he stopped getting paid to play basketball he spent the rest of his working years as a hunting guide in some of America's wildest places.

Viewed as a whole, Kenny Sailors's life story is a tale of basketball and the outdoors, and of Wyoming and Alaska.

—LEW FREEDMAN, AUGUST 2013

CHAPTER 1

The Jump Shot's Beginnings

THE BOYS WERE BEST FRIENDS, yet also rivals on the basketball court. Bud was the older brother and he was much taller than younger brother Kenny. Almost every day they went out to the backyard of their Hillsdale, Wyoming, home and shot the round ball at the round hoop on the hard-packed dirt court.

Eventually, following a bit of practice and loosening up, they began playing games against one another. This was one-on-one basketball, usually the scores going to twenty-one. Always, always, Bud was the winner. In 1934, with Bud in high school and Kenny a thirteen-year-old in junior high, Bud stood about ten inches taller than his younger sibling. There was little Kenny could do on defense to stop Bud when he put his mind to scoring.

Similarly, when Bud wanted to stop Kenny from scoring he used his superior size and muscle to push him away from the basket and sometimes swat his shot attempt into the fields where they grew the food that sustained the small family during the 1930s Great Depression era when cash was scarce.

Kenny and Bud grew up on a small ranch with their mother, Cora, that had no telephone or running water. It was the way much of America lived in the 1930s outside of major cities and especially during the Depression. Their father went missing from the family picture by their formative years, and times were definitely tough when America faced the most devastating economic slowdown in its history. The Depression threw people out of work by the millions and affected almost every living American's daily existence.

Kenny Sailors was actually born in Bushnell, Nebraska, on January 14, 1921, in the southwest corner of the state. The Sailors clan lived on a ranch in the

work days on the farm. "We had harrows, plows, and cultivators and they were all designed for horses. We used those to farm and we always planted between twenty and forty acres of potatoes. That's a lot of half-mile rows."

Initially, the hardest work chores fell to Bud because he was older, bigger, and stronger than Kenny. Bud did most of the cultivating with the horses and Kenny and his mother did the hoeing. It was their job to scrape out the weeds.

"Bud could get the weeds on each side of the potatoes in the row, but the ones in the middle he couldn't reach," Sailors said. "The ones that were real close to the potatoes we had to pull out by hand. We couldn't chop them out or else we would chop out the potato vines."

By the time Sailors was ten years old he had learned that there were no free rides in this world, that he would have to work hard to succeed or to get anywhere in life. There came a time as a boy, though, when he did express doubt about all of that sweating and bending and hoeing.

"I'll never forget one morning after we had been doing this for a month straight when I was nine or ten and I was tired of it," Sailors said. "I was always hungry and thirsty. I can't remember a time when I wasn't hungry back then. I said something to my mother and I don't know what I was thinking, but anyway I said, 'Mom, I'm getting awfully tired of this hoeing. We've been doing it a long time now.' She said, 'I know son, but these potatoes are what make us the money to live off. We've got to hoe the weeds out.' I should have shut up then, but I didn't. I said it again. 'Well, I'm getting awful tired. I just don't like it.'"

It might be said with confidence that young Kenny Sailors was not envisioning a life as a farmer.

Sailors probably realized at that moment that he had gone too far because his mother greeted his second pronouncement with a long pause. Her silence indicated she had given considerable thought to her next comment.

Cora said, "Well, Kenneth, just take your hoe and go to the house if that's the way you feel." Kenny's mother always used his first name in addressing him, not necessarily as an expression of anger. The combination of the words and the tone of voice did not sound quite right to Kenny.

"Something was wrong," he said. "I started to go with my hoe, but I was moving pretty slow." And then she said, 'Just don't come to the dinner table tonight.' She meant it. No dinner. I probably wouldn't have had any breakfast, either, until I went out and did some more hoeing. That was my mother. Boy, I tell you, I grabbed that hoe and went at it. I never said another word about it the rest of the summer. We hoed weeds, my mother and I, all forty acres of those weeds. It took us some time, but we did it."

The Sailors boys worked very hard under Cora's supervision, but when they did get some free time they chose to fill the hours, or minutes, with basketball. Bud's given name was Barton and while Kenny always said that he was a good brother to him the bigger boy did not take it easy in competitions against his sibling.

When Kenny was thirteen he stood about 5-foot-6 or so. Bud was already in high school and had filled out to nearly 6-foot-5. Some people said he was the tallest person for miles around. The size difference is why Kenny was always on the losing end of those basketball contests. Bud was going to make Kenny work to beat him and he did not envision his younger brother dreaming up such a surprising plan with the use of a secret weapon in order to do so.

"It was just a weapon that came naturally," Kenny said of his first jump shot. "He was big, but he was fast enough to stop my drive."

One day Kenny just got fed up with losing every single one-on-one game of hoops to big brother. When his turn came to play offense rather than drive directly at Bud for an attempted layup, one that quite possibly might be swatted into the potato rows, he stopped in place, jumped in the air, and shot the ball in a high arc toward the hoop. At various times over the years, Kenny has said the first jumper went in and at other times he has said he can't remember. It's a better story if the shot is accompanied by a swish, but in the big picture it doesn't really matter.

The jump shot was born that day. The jump shot was born out of necessity and frustration.

In the world of basketball, there are casual references to a player's creativity as being "a playground move." That essentially has grown to mean that a dazzling maneuver with the ball was something daring that might not be tried in a structured game. For the time period of the 1930s and long after, a jump shot would be considered a radical play and not one approved of for regular use by most high school or college coaches.

Although they also have come to be accepted stylish plays in the sport of basketball, other early examples (though not nearly that early) would be a behind-the-back pass in the flow of a game, or the crossover dribble. In the 1930s and 1940s such plays would be far too fancy for the taste of traditional coaches. In the 1950s, the Boston Celtic's star playmaker, Bob Cousy, became the first NBA point guard to regularly throw behind-the-back passes. As time went by such clever passes became somewhat routine for the best players and far more sophisticated ball handling evolved in the 1950s, 1960s, and right on up to the present. Fans and teammates applaud the effective use of those kinds of efforts, but even now they are still not taken for granted when used to score points.

There were certainly times during the evolution of those flashy plays when coaches frowned on their use and at the time Sailors became the only jump shooter around there were those who distinctly discouraged trying it.

"If your feet left the floor," Sailors said of shooting the ball seventy and more years ago, "you were a freak. You were on the bench. It's hard for people to believe."

In the truest sense of the description, Kenny Sailors's first jump shot against his brother, Bud, was a playground move. It was about survival and playing to win, and so he dug into a bag of tricks that wasn't even a bag, but a single magical play that evened up the odds between him and his opponent.

Most assuredly, Bud Sailors, who went on to play high school and college basketball in Wyoming before an Air Force career that culminated with the rank of colonel, was surprised by his brother's slick offensive shot.

"We played quite a bit before he figured out he could dribble and get that one-handed shot on me," Bud said while reminiscing in 1988. "That was the first time I'd run into it. I was almost 6-5 already. I don't care how tall you are, you're either going to foul him or he's going to make it. He was real accurate with it."

Kenny Sailors never for a moment thought during his childhood that his jump shot would become his signature play, that it would aid him in getting to college, and would enable him to become a professional athlete. His goals were modest—he just wanted to score on Bud. It was quite satisfying when Bud could not stop the shot.

Bud and Kenny really weren't playing actual games on the playground. They played by themselves on their backyard, makeshift court. They lived in such a rural environment that they really didn't have any boys around of their age to play basketball against when they got their free time. The closest neighbors lived a half mile away.

The home Kenny and Bud grew up in was a two-story structure that Kenny called "a rambling ranch house." When they were small they shared a bed together, but as they grew they slept in their own beds, though in the same room. Bud grew fast and protested that there wasn't enough room for both of them in a single bed anymore.

Fairly large, especially on the second floor, the house was on the older side and when the wind blew across the open plains, holes in its façade were exposed and let in exceptionally cold air.

"Wintertime you could look right out and see the daylight through the cracks," Sailors said. "That wind, man oh man. Mom just piled more big old comforters on us. She made those quilts a few inches thick. If we said we were cold she gave us another comforter."

Young Kenny Sailors wore his hair tightly cropped as a youth, what would later be called a crew cut, or was viewed as a military cut and his hairstyle has rarely changed throughout his life. Neither Cora Sailors, nor Kenny, was much interested in seeing him with long hair. For a little while when he was playing in college and in the pros Kenny actually wore his hair wavier and long enough to comb, but the fashion he stuck with most of his life was pretty much the short cut he grew up with. Another habit he acquired young was reading from the Bible. Cora read verses to her sons each night, some of what she said aloud stuck, and the idea of doing it did stick with Kenny. Throughout his life he periodically just took out a Bible at home and read from it.

Although as an athlete he grew in muscularity, Sailors has also been fairly slender throughout most of his life, too. As a little boy there was no fat on him, as a ballplayer there was no fat on him, and as he aged he kept most of the fat off through exercise. Interest in the outdoors was ingrained in Sailors early in life. There were no fancy games like Nintendo or electronic games when he was growing up and there wasn't much indoors besides a good meal that interested Kenny and Bud.

The Sailors boys didn't even listen to the radio much at all. They were pretty much outside, whether it was working on the farm, playing basketball, or while Kenny was learning how to hunt.

The first animal Sailors pursued was the jackrabbit common to areas of the West. Jackrabbits are hares, not directly connected to the types of bunny rabbits often kept as pets by youngsters. They are speedier than 100-meter dash men in the Olympics and their fantastic jumps exceed the abilities of NBA players with memorable vertical leaps. They are also larger than the typical rabbit.

"I used to go out and hunt rabbits," Sailors said of when he was around ten years old. "I didn't even have a gun at first. I used to just chase them with my hound dog. In those days the owners of fox farms would pay you twenty-five cents, or something like that, for a rabbit. The reason I didn't have a gun at first was because my mother wouldn't let me have one."

While it was quite common for boys coming of age in the West at that time to shoot .22-caliber rifles, Sailors was first saddled with a completely different type of instrument at mom's insistence. She wanted him to learn how to play the violin.

"My heart wasn't in it," Sailors admitted. "She finally became so disgusted after a few lessons, and so did the guy giving me the lessons, that she said all right, forget it." One reason that Sailors might have been disenchanted with the violin, he learned later, was that he didn't even have the proper ear for the music. "There are certain notes on the violin I couldn't even hear. Must have been fate, I think. I could certainly hear the sound a gun made when it went off. I bet my violin playing was so bad the sounds I made sliding that bow across the strings would have caused any bear or sheep to surrender if they'd heard it. I never would have needed a rifle."

Sure enough, by the time Sailors was twelve, he was retired from violin playing. Cora sold the musical instrument and bought a .22 for him with the money. After that Sailors and his hound dog had an ally in the chase for jackrabbits. The rifle was more than an equalizer. At first Sailors could not hit a rabbit on the run, but only sitting, but he developed into a crack shot. The jackrabbits that were not sold to the fox farms ended up on the dinner table.

"They made good mincemeat," Sailors said. "Mom made mincemeat pies out of them. We'd eat the jackrabbits in the springtime and I'd sell them in the winter when they weren't so good to eat. They were thinner. They were easier to spot in the winter, though. Out along the fence line you could spot them in the snow. Those twenty-five-cent payoffs kept me in ammunition, anyway."

Hunting was a way of life in the Sailors family, especially during the Depression when cash was dear and the best way to feed the trio was growing crops on the farm and hunting meat in the woods. Everything from squirrels to jackrabbits, to chickens, yes, chickens, were shot.

"Anything that wasn't a varmint," Sailors said.

When it was time to serve chicken as a main course, Cora Sailors didn't bother with an axe. She was such a fine shot, an Annie Oakley with a purpose, that when a chicken's number was up she simply stood out in the yard and shot the unlucky chicken's head off from a distance.

"She'd just take that .22 and get him," Sailors said. "Boom!"

Sailors was still little and he hadn't yet earned trust with a rifle, but once in a while he was assigned to catch an animal by hand and bring it home for dinner. Sailors remembers one time in particular when he and his mother were picking corn in the field on a Saturday, a day off from school. The corn was actually to feed the hogs, and sometimes a cow, but not the people. It was hard work picking the corn and throwing it high over an adjacent row since the corn stalks looked twelve feet high to a kid. The corn would fly over a row and be deposited in a hay rack pulled by horses.

"It was a team of gentle horses," Sailors said. "They just walked down the rows. Mom would holler, 'Giddyup!' and they go a couple of feet and she would say, 'Whoa!' and they'd stop. We did that for a half a mile. My old hound dog was with us and it seemed like it chased a rabbit out of a hole. Mom said, 'Kenneth, you get over there and find that hound of yours and see if he's bringing that rabbit in. Catch him when he gets close enough. She didn't think I'd catch a big, old jackrabbit in a million years."

But that didn't mean Sailors wasn't going to try. First he discovered which row the dog and rabbit were sprinting down. It was about three rows over.

"When the rabbit got up close, I could see him," Sailors said. "His ears were laid back flat on his head, his eyes were rolled back and he was watching for that hound dog. He wasn't looking ahead. That sucker ran right into my hands and I grabbed him. Mom couldn't believe it. My biggest problem was the hound dog. He was so excited he was about to eat me and the rabbit."

Cora began shouting to her son, "Hang on to him, Kenneth! Hang on to him! We'll cook him." It was quite the helter-skelter scene. Mom reached Sailors first, ahead of the dog, seized the rabbit by its hind legs and it was all over quickly.

"The easiest thing in the world to do to kill a rabbit, or anything, is by grabbing it just behind the neck," Sailors said. "My mom took that rabbit home, skinned him out, cleaned him all up, and boiled him in hot water until the meat was cooked. She made mincemeat pie out of it. The young ones, boy, they taste just like chicken."

If Sailors had somehow become proficient in playing the violin there is a chance he never would have migrated to Alaska because much of his living on The Last Frontier revolved around guiding hunts.

Sailors learned to shoot the rifle the same way he learned to take the jump shot—mostly on his own. Bud gave him the basic introductory instruction and then he practiced. He became quite good at making both types of shots.

"Shooting a rifle is like anything else," Sailors said. "You've got to practice to be any good at it. I spent many hours shooting jump shots on the basketball court. Over and over. It was the same with hunting weapons."

Growing up during the Depression and learning to hunt to put meat on the table taught Sailors lessons that he applied to his hunting guide life in Alaska years later. Whether it was seeking big game for trophies, as some of his clients wished, or hunting for food, one thing would not be tolerated—no wasted meat.

"It's terrible to kill an animal just for fun," Sailors said, "for no purpose, and to let it lie in the grass and rot just because you don't want to carry the meat out, or because you don't think its rack is big enough. There are laws against that. In Alaska, the state Department of Fish and Game will hit you with a big fine—several thousand dollars—if you are caught wasting an animal or violating other hunting rules like taking an animal out of season. In all my years of guiding in Wyoming or Alaska I was never cited for a violation. I respected the animals we hunted. I knew there would be no future for the guiding profession if we were to wantonly waste the animals the way they treated buffalo in the early days. Waste is a sin. People who lived through the Depression years understand this."

It was a bus ride to attend elementary school, and in the sparsely populated Hillsdale School District the elementary and junior highs combined only mustered about forty children. The school was tiny and that impacted what types of sports were available for kids to play. There weren't enough boys to field a serious football team, which was too expensive to outfit, anyway. Basketball was the thing in Hillsdale where it took only five on a side to compete.

"Basketball was all they had," Sailors said.

Little towns like Hillsdale pockmarked the landscape. Many of them were located near the railroad that crossed the state, but the residents had farming and basketball in common because none of them could field teams in sports like football or baseball that required many players or expensive gear. Egbert, Carpenter, Burns, Chugwater, and Pine Bluff were all Hillsdale rivals.

Although Kenny Sailors may have gravitated toward playing basketball anyway since it was essentially the only game in town, Bud's involvement in the sport and interest in it sparked Kenny's initial passion. If the older brother he idolized was playing basketball, it must have been all right.

It was Bud who erected the backyard hoop on a windmill. Bud was in high school by the time Kenny reached junior high, and he wanted to practice and

Kenny (right) with his brother Barton "Bud" in Falls City, Nebraska, in front of their grandfather's store, circa 1926. (Photo courtesy Kenny Sailors.)

practice. The court itself was dirt, packed-down dirt. It was often dusty in the area and Bud watered down the dirt and then swept off any loose dirt to create a firm surface.

Older and always taller, by the time the Sailors brothers began playing their one-on-one games Bud was not only closing in on his final height of 6-5, he was a very good player.

"My brother was the best basketball player in that whole area," Kenny Sailors said. "He was the big shot in that whole league. He tried to convince me that basketball wasn't going to be my game because I was too small."

The only other sport Kenny might have tried in school at that time was track and field. Despite the lack of encouragement from Bud, Kenny never gave serious thought to quitting basketball.

At that point in the evolution of the sport any time a basket was scored the ball was taken to midcourt for a center jump. It was a tedious way to play the game and eventually the rules were adjusted, but the frequency of jump balls did not reward the kind of speed that Kenny Sailors possessed. In fact, since that rule pretty much eliminated the fast break, it rendered Sailors's quickness irrelevant much of the time.

"Bud couldn't see a little guy like me doing much in that kind of a game," Sailors said. "I could understand why. He really meant it. He thought I was just too much of a runt, as he called me. That kind of irritated me, though he was a good brother to me in most ways. Playing in the backyard with Bud is where I learned to play and when the school bus picked us up in wintertime for the seven or eight miles into Hillsdale, the first thing we did was make a run for the gym."

The gym teacher or coach left the basketballs out in the gym for the kids to play and shoot around before class started. If Sailors developed the jump shot out of need when going up against big brother, he developed his deft skill dribbling the ball in what would pass for disorganized mayhem during those pre-school sessions.

There might be ten or twelve kids wanting to play, but rather than form squads to play games and keep score the pre-school sessions evolved into keep-away games. The agreed-upon rules said that any player who got hold of the ball could keep it as long as he could dribble it without having it taken away by the others. So Kenny Sailors, who would become a world-class dribbler, honed that skill in that peculiar manner.

"A kid would grab the basketball and could keep dribbling it," Sailors said. "It was your ball, but the minute you quit dribbling it, you had to give it up. That's where I learned to dribble so well. You get six or seven guys chasing you and trying to take the ball away from you and you couldn't stop. If you picked it up, you were done, so you had to keep dribbling.

"Eventually, someone was going to swat it away from you, but I got to where

I was pretty good at that, the best of the bunch. I could dribble that ball longer than the rest of them. We had the whole gym to run in and all these guys would chase you to get that ball from you."

Given that the game was not football, nor rugby, the player could not tuck the ball under an arm and run with it. It was hectic and crazy and the kind of fun youngsters like to indulge in, but the challenge of it turned Sailors into a superior ball handler.

"We made our own rules, but we played by them," he said. "I look back on that and those days had a lot to do with teaching me to dribble the ball and they taught me how to take contact and still control the ball. They would knock you down practically, and jump on you, and everything, but you had to keep dribbling."

Later, when he was playing competitive ball in high school, college, and the NBA, Kenny Sailors, the runt, would take all sorts of hits from big men guarding the hoop, but he shrugged them off and he could still score on those guys. He either sank that jump shot over their outstretched arms, or dribbled past them for layups. The lessons of his youth on the playground at home and in the gym at school stayed with him for a lifetime.

CHAPTER 2

Becoming a Player

KENNY SAILORS ADMITS THAT HIS FIRST RUDIMENTARY ATTEMPTS to develop a jump shot were rough around the edges. Later, when he was a star player at the University of Wyoming, he possessed the picture-perfect form employing the shot that all basketball fans have come to admire for its smoothness.

However, as a junior high kid going up against his much bigger brother he was a work in progress. Not surprisingly because he had no role models to pattern his shot after. Not only was there no film to study, there was no one to study. Sailors had no predecessor to copy. His jump shot came about through trial and error.

"You didn't see the jump shot," Sailors said. "I wasn't shooting it with the wrist and fingers the way I did later. Little kids tend to shoot from their hip and I'm sure that I used my body a lot. That was the idea, to protect the shot from Bud. I would say that I didn't even develop my jump shot to just the way I wanted it until my senior year in college."

One thing Sailors did not lack was dedication. Mostly he shot baskets by himself. Often it was he and Bud going hard against one another in their personal rivalry contests. Wyoming is not regarded as a tropical paradise and oftentimes the weather conspired against them when they had free time. They ignored it. They played those backyard games regardless of climate. Sometimes that meant playing in the snow. Hillsdale was in flat country and the wind roared across the prairie at a howl with nothing to stop it, or even to slow it down. It didn't matter. The boys played ball.

Still, even after Kenny created his jump shot and realized Bud couldn't block it, he couldn't beat big brother in games to twenty-one. Bud could always score on the much smaller Kenny.

"I never beat him," Kenny said. "He was five years older than me. My jump shot wasn't developed enough yet, either. That didn't come until later."

That wind was memorable and sometimes it was a marvel that it didn't gather the strength to blow the Union Pacific cars right off the railroad line when it howled. It should not be terribly surprising that Sailors's roots, the ranch house and the windmill, were battered by so much weather that they eventually came apart, disintegrated, and disappeared.

In late 2011, some of Sailors's late-in-life friends wanted to see where he grew up and developed that jump shot. They took a drive from Laramie, where the university is located, to Hillsdale, but there wasn't much left to see.

"I don't think anything at all of the buildings are left," is how Sailors summed up the site with a lack of surprise. "We're talking about eighty years ago. But that's where I started. My brother did give me a lot of help. He talked to me a lot, gave me advice."

Also, by the time Sailors began playing for a school team at the junior high level, the rules had changed, had been loosened up. No more did teams have to truck to the center of the court for a jump ball after every basket. Now the team that had just been scored on could pass the ball in and bring it up-court. That increased the speed and flexibility of the game and played to Sailors's strengths. For a player blessed with quick hands, exquisite dribbling skills, and fast feet, the new style was a good match.

"That changed the whole context of the game," Sailors said. "That's when Bud decided that hey, a [short] kid could play in a game like this."

The first basketball team that Sailors played on was Hillsdale's junior high club. He was a good player immediately, but still very much learning team dynamics and the nuances of the sport. Hillsdale's schooling ran out after eighth grade. Cora wanted her boys to attend college, so she gave up the rural lifestyle and the family moved into a new home in Laramie. That was the end of farming, but the new house was large enough to accommodate not only her, Bud, and Kenny, but to take in boarders and that's what she did to make money.

Sailors said the house, on Fifth Street in Laramie, had perhaps seven or eight rooms in the upstairs and the size enabled the family to make a good living from rentals. It was located close to the University of Wyoming and the specialty of the house was renting to college students looking for off-campus living.

"She took in college kids and boarded and roomed them," Sailors said. "She did it a lot cheaper than they could get it anywhere else. But we had a bunch of them."

By then Bud was old enough for college and he enrolled at Wyoming. He was a good enough player to make the basketball team, too. And Kenny was a good enough player to make the team at Laramie High School. At the time the city just had one high school, though it has grown sufficiently to support others now.

Back then the school had a rule against freshmen playing on the varsity, so in ninth grade he was limited to competing for a spot on the freshman-only team. Sailors tried out, made the team, and became a starter at guard. Sailors was still shooting his jump shot, but it was viewed as somewhat reckless play and he was not encouraged. It was anathema to jump and shoot at the same time because it was felt that diminished accuracy. The set shot was a proven commodity. Why tamper with that?

"I didn't shoot it much because the coaches didn't like it," Sailors said. "They didn't want you leaving the floor on offense or defense."

At the time the only acceptable time to leap during a game was if a player was going after a rebound. Otherwise, it was philosophically taboo.

The next year, Sailors's sophomore year, he moved onto the varsity and jump-shooting inclinations or not, he became a backcourt starter. Laramie High School was pretty good, but the team lacked size and that held it back from being championship caliber.

"We were just about average," Sailors said. "We didn't have a bunch of big men, just a bunch of little runts like me."

By Sailors's junior year the Plainsmen were more than average. The team was very good. Sailors was the leading scorer and he was chosen All-State for the first time, one of those accomplishments that sticks on a resume for as long as a ballplayer stays in the game and something that is always fondly remembered. As a team Laramie belied its lack of height, making up for it with skill and speed, and ran through the state tournament to the championship game.

"We were beat by Rock Springs in the finals," Sailors said.

That's how the 1938 season ended. Rock Springs was a power at the time and that school's victory marked a third straight title.

His senior year was almost the instant replay. Sailors was very fast and he had good spring in his legs—he won a state championship in the long jump, too. He was the team's leader on the court, the leading scorer in the box scores, and the squad again blitzed through the state tournament until reaching the championship contest. This time, in 1939, the title-game foe was Casper, but again the Plainsmen lost.

"My senior year it was the same thing," Sailors said. "We got beat in the last thirty seconds of the game by a crazy shot. So we came in second both times." Sailors was also chosen All-State for a second time.

In high school, where Sailors was faster than almost all of his opponents and could out-dribble most of them, most of his points came on drives to the basket beating the defense. More often than not when he took an outside shot it was a set shot rather than a jumper. He knew his coach, Floyd Foreman, and the assistants, disliked the jumper and seemed uncomfortable any time he left his feet, so he conformed to what they wanted, and did not push the envelope to do what felt comfortable.

"I was the top scorer on the team, but most of what I did was driving or set shots," Sailors said. "I shot a jump shot once in a while, but I was afraid to shoot too many of them. I knew the coaches didn't like it. My coach was a good coach, and he never did say anything to me, but I knew that all coaches frowned on leaving your feet when you shot. So I didn't do it too much. But I shot some jump shots. Still, more and more I kept trying to develop different things on offense."

Although Sailors was an all-star performer and was the Plainsmen's leading scorer, that did not mean he lit it up the way present-day high school stars do. The game was much slower in the 1930s and to the best of his recollection, as a senior Sailors averaged about 12 points a game.

In 1939, the University of Wyoming, which was a mere full-court pass away from Sailors's home, hired a new basketball coach named Everett Shelton. Shelton, who was originally from Kansas, was already a mature man, not a fledgling coach. He was born in 1898 and besides a long tenure leading the Cowboys, Shelton also coached in high school, Amateur Athletic Union (AAU) ball, and at Sacramento State.

The world of college basketball was vastly different in 1939 than it is in the 2000s. The first NCAA championship tournament was conducted that year, one season after the National Invitation Tournament (NIT) was founded. The two events provided the sport with its first national championship recognition.

Oregon defeated Ohio State, 46-33, in the first NCAA title game in 1939 at Northwestern University. It took decades, but the NCAA tournament gradually overtook and eclipsed the NIT in prestige and the event became one of the most popular on the American sporting scene.

Another major difference—a huge difference—is the way current high school players are wooed and chased, wined and dined and inundated with communications from coaches begging them to attend their schools and enhance the quality of their basketball program. There was no recruiting mail being sent when Sailors completed high school.

There is no doubt that Shelton knew who Kenny Sailors was. He was, after all, the biggest star on the Laramie High School team, twice All-State, and showing his stuff on a nightly basis throughout a couple of winters just down the street. Likewise, Sailors knew who Shelton was, if not very much about him.

The idea of attending college was appealing and Wyoming was right there. Sailors never thought of attending another institution and no other college approached him with the suggestion that he come on down and play basketball for it.

"Nobody ever recruited me," Sailors said.

It might be a slight exaggeration to say that Sailors really knew who Shelton was. Shelton was new to the neighborhood and was just introducing himself to Cowboys fans. His background was in AAU ball and he had led a team to a national amateur championship before turning to college ball.

"He hadn't been there long," Sailors said, "and nobody knew what a great coach he really was. He knew the game of basketball. He came from AAU play, coaching Phillips 66 and the Denver Safeways. He didn't have anything to do with college ball until he got to Wyoming."

Before the National Basketball Association was created in the late 1940s and took root (and even afterward for a while in the 1950s) many of the top college basketball players who wished to continue competing after graduation joined AAU clubs. During the season they represented an employer in basketball and during the off-season, and after they retired, they held down jobs at a company and established careers. Technically, they remained amateurs and thus eligible for Olympic play because ostensibly they were being paid for their jobs, not their play. For many years, playing AAU ball provided more money and security than playing for an NBA team, though that was no longer true by the 1960s.

Compared to the NBA and NCAA play, Amateur Athletic Union basketball history is grossly overlooked. Beginning in 1920, the AAU selected All-American teams and they were prestigious. Between 1920 and 1968, thirty-three players from AAU teams represented the United States in the Summer Olympics and won gold medals. The most famous AAU team of the time was the Phillips 66, out of Bartlesville, Oklahoma. Military teams also played in AAU competition.

Hank Luisetti, known for his one-handed shot, though not an actual jump shot as is recognized today, twice was chosen as an AAU All-American while representing the San Francisco Olympic Club. Sailors himself was named an AAU All-American for the 1942–43 season although he was still part of the University of Wyoming team.

"Shelton won some in AAU ball," Sailors said. "People today don't have a clue how big-time AAU basketball was in that day. It was bigger than college. These were players who had made All-American teams in college. They played on some corporation or company team for six, eight, or ten years."

Mostly overlooked in Sailors's athletic career was how when he got the chance to play the sport in high school he blossomed as a football player. He was a novice at the game because his elementary/junior high school did not have a team, but when he showed up in Laramie he thrived at the game.

It turned out with his fleet feet and good hands, Sailors was a very good end. In those days players went both ways, on offense and defense, and Sailors didn't mind the contact required in hitting people either. He was good enough as an offensive and defensive end to be selected All-State in football, too.

Sailors had not been recruited to play college basketball and enrolled at Wyoming without any particular encouragement that he was going to be suiting up for the Cowboy hoopsters. He wanted to continue his football education, too, so it was no secret that he intended to go out for the college team, even though he weighed just 138 pounds at the time.

Sailors did not consider his slight stature to be a handicap because he had run rings around 240 pounders in high school.

"I played offense, defense, special teams, any way, we all did," Sailors said. "It didn't bother me. I didn't have any trouble in high school with the bigger guys. I'd just get out of their way or push them over. I was fast and quick. I planned to go out for football and basketball, which you could do with the shorter seasons in those days."

Even after school began freshman student Kenny Sailors had never met Everett Shelton. It was at that point that Shelton injected himself into Sailors's life.

"Shelton, the new coach, came around to me and said, 'Sailors, they tell me that you're going to go out for football,'" Sailors recalled. "I started to tell him how good I was in football and he said, 'I know all about that. You were

All-State a couple of years. I know that. But if you're going to go out for football, just forget about basketball.'"

Sailors was dismayed to receive that ultimatum. He wanted some advice from someone he trusted, but it felt as if there was no one he could discuss that issue with. Brother Bud was already gone from Wyoming and was in the service. It didn't seem as if his mother Cora would be a good sounding board.

"That surprised me," Sailors said of Shelton laying down his personal law. "I didn't have anybody to go to." Not that there was any kind of appeals process. "He meant it."

Very little publicity about Sailors's high school football career is readily accessible, but one newspaper clipping that was just five paragraphs long reported the shellacking of the Plainsmen 45–6 by Sheridan. The final paragraph reads, "Kenny Sailors, Laramie end, was easily the best lineman on the field. He fought viciously and checked the Indians' power sweeps time and time again." A short boldfaced note, not attributed to any sports writer, like the game report itself, read, "Gentlemen notice: How about this Kenny Sailors, Laramie end, for all-state consideration—a bearcat if ever there was one."

A Laramie roster of the time indicated that Sailors wore No. 30 as a player and weighed 140 pounds. It was probably rounded up from that 138 pounds mentioned, which may have sounded too puny.

Although basketball had been Sailors's first sporting love and he had demonstrated a talent for the game, he felt he was just beginning to understand his potential as a football player and was reluctant to let it go. Still not completely at ease with making the call on his own, Sailors sought out Floyd Foreman, his old high school basketball coach.

"He was a good friend of mine and was one of the best coaches I ever played for," Sailors said. "He and Shelton were the two best coaches I ever played for, not just because they were my coaches, but because they were both good men."

Foreman did have a sympathetic ear, yet a realistic outlook. He listened to Sailors lament the situation, that he had to make a choice, but he thought of him as a basketball player.

"I went to Coach Foreman and I said, 'Coach,'" Sailors relayed, "'Do you know what that new coach up at the university told me? He said if I was going to go out for football, to forget about basketball.'

"My old high school coach kind of turned his head away from me so I couldn't see his face clearly and I bet he was kind of smiling a little," Sailors said. "He said, 'Well, you know Kenny, you only weigh 138 pounds. That's not real heavy for college football.' I'd never even thought of it because I never got hurt playing high school football and they used to tackle as hard as anyone.

"That's what he told me. I said. 'What should I do?' He hesitated for a little while and said, 'You know, Kenny, I think I'd listen to him.'"

Sailors listened to both coaches and from the hindsight of decades of perspective he knows he made the right call.

"Boy, I'm glad I did," he said. "You never can tell what would have happened. I might have gotten bumped up my first year of football and ruined my basketball. I understand it today, but I didn't understand it at the time because I was a good football player in high school. I had also learned a lot from football. I learned how to handle contact without it bothering me, and that really pulled me through in college basketball with the players all being bigger and stronger. My mentality was to just get to the basket, and I didn't worry about how hard I got hit by somebody."

While Sailors's trademark is the jump shot as a player those who watched him would probably rank his ability to drive to the hoop as an equal offensive weapon. Shelton stressed that he should always be looking for a sliver of space to dribble through and take advantage of a defensive weakness and Sailors shined at that part of the game. It seemed he could dribble through the eye of a needle. As the playmaker, he controlled where the ball went on offense, and often enough it stayed in his hands when he spied the opportunity of open space.

"I had a coach [Shelton] who pounded it into my head to get to the basket, whatever you do," Sailors said. "If you get the foul along with it, that's fine, but get to the basket. That's what I worked on. In practice, every place, get to that basket. It paid off for me, not just in college, but even in the pros. I could get past most guys with my dribble, especially, bigger, slower guys who I could blow right past. I had a few fakes, too. I became known for the jump shot, but my drives to the basket were just as important."

Most of the people who came to know Kenny Sailors in college, as an NBA player, in Alaska, and later in life, probably don't even know that he flirted with playing college football. For Sailors, the story of his athletic life was mapped out in the moment he selected basketball over football at the University of Wyoming. As in the famous Robert Frost poem, for Sailors football was the road not taken. Basketball became his life path.

CHAPTER 3

Wyoming Hoops

OVER THE DECADES THE NCAA has swung back and forth like a pendulum with its policy of allowing freshman to play varsity sports immediately upon enrolling in college and not letting them play until their sophomore year of school. The theory behind prohibiting a freshman from competing on the varsity right away is that it will be easier for him to settle into school before taking on a demanding extracurricular activity. It has been a waxing and waning policy and right now freshmen are eligible to compete right away. Not when Kenny Sailors showed up for college at Wyoming in the fall of 1939, though.

That applied if Sailors had played football or basketball, or both. As a freshman he was earmarked for the freshman basketball team once he discarded his ambition to play both sports. That meant a player could compete for only three varsity seasons, not four.

"They just didn't think freshmen should be playing varsity ball," Sailors said. "There weren't many freshmen. The school was pretty small then, maybe two thousand students full- and part-time, not like now (when enrollment is around thirteen thousand). It wasn't a big college like it is now. The freshmen worked out with the varsity players and scrimmaged against them."

The freshman team also had its own schedule. This particular group of freshmen was pretty cocky and they were convinced they were already better than the more experienced varsity. They were not shy about expressing their opinion, either.

"Coach Shelton got tired of us kidding and razzing his varsity team about

27

how we could beat them," Sailors said. "We thought we could. We knew we could because we played against them in practice every day."

Sailors may have grown up on the prairie and had his growth in the game stifled a little bit by the prejudice against using the jump shot, but by the time he became a Cowboy he was far more confident and capable. He knew that he had the speed to blow right past the big men on the varsity and take the ball to the hoop and he was sure the varsity players understood that, too, even if Shelton was not yet in the know.

"I could go past some of them so fast I'd create a breeze and they'd catch a cold," Sailors said. "The old coach evidently wasn't that much aware of it. We knew we were as good or better than they were and we kidded them about it a lot. Shelton got tired of it and said, 'You crazy freshmen. If you really think you can beat the varsity we'll schedule a game and you can play against them and see how great you are.'"

Sailors said Shelton was positive that the varsity would wipe the floor with the freshmen players, but he underestimated his youngest players.

"It just tickled us to death when he scheduled the game," Sailors said. "We knew we could beat them and we didn't just beat them, we throttled them."

This was no private encounter in the practice gym with the stands empty, either. When Shelton said he would schedule a game he meant it. Played in the main auditorium, the game was advertised and tickets were sold. More than five thousand people attended, enticed by the Freshman Versus Varsity touting. The Wyoming newspapers that ordinarily covered the Cowboys games were captivated by the matchup.

Shelton explained why he was doing it—to show the freshmen they were not quite the big hotshots they might have thought they were.

"We drew a crowd and we beat them quite handily," Sailors said.

Not only did the result shut up the varsity, but it quieted Shelton, too. It also encouraged him. For the first time he seemed to comprehend the talent he had on the freshman squad that was going to be moving up to the varsity the next winter.

"He didn't say much afterwards," Sailors said of Shelton. "But his whole attitude seemed to change towards the freshmen. Then he finally made a statement to someone about the game and it got back to us. He said, 'I didn't realize those freshmen were as good as ballplayers as they are. They're pretty good.'"

A bond was forged between the freshmen when they played together that winter and they progressed through school at the same rate. Jim Weir, Lew

Roney, and Floyd Volker, all of whom are now deceased, along with Sailors, formed the core of the Cowboys varsity in the coming years.

As a freshman Sailors was still hesitant to shoot his jump shot as often as he would have liked, but he did step up its usage rate from high school. Shelton never sought to discourage its use, never talked to Sailors in a disparaging way about how the jump shot meant taking off-balance shots at the basket, or how it was silly to jump in the air to shoot.

"He never tried to stop me," Sailors said. "He must have seen something in it. He never tried to show me a better way to shoot. I don't think he knew too much about jump shooting. I don't think any of the coaches did."

The gang of four from the freshman team formed friendships out of their shared experiences and became the nucleus of Wyoming's greatest team. All four of them were Wyoming bred and came out of Wyoming high school basketball programs. Weir was a 6-foot-6 forward from Green River.

"Weir was the best big man that Wyoming had had up until that point," Sailors said. "He was fast and quick."

Roney was from Powell, Wyoming. Volker was from Casper. Volker, who stood 6-foot-4, was like Sailors able to forge a professional basketball career after completing his eligibility at Wyoming and after the conclusion of World War II. He played in the National Basketball League and then during the early days of the fledgling NBA for the Indianapolis Olympians and the original Denver Nuggets.

Sailors was probably closer to Volker than the others, but said they were all friends.

"Volker was a good friend of mine," he said. "They all were. Sometimes we socialized together. Not a lot. But we went to the movies or fishing a time or two."

Shelton was a new face in Laramie when he took over the Cowboys for the 1939–40 season and whether he would admit it or not to the freshmen, his varsity wasn't particularly good that year. The club finished just 6–10. But Shelton was already a fairly famous coach with some serious credentials on his resume. He guided the Denver Safeways to an AAU crown in 1937 and he was viewed as a pioneer for his innovative leadership developing the five-man weave offense.

"Shelton's Weave" many called the half-court offensive plan that he implemented upon arrival in Wyoming and which his second-year team, with Sailors guiding the offense, began to perfect. Shelton, who won 850 games as a

Everett Shelton, the coach and mastermind of the 1942-43 University of Wyoming NCAA basketball team and the coach that Kenny Sailors said is the best he ever played for. (Photo courtesy the University of Wyoming.)

coach at all levels of the sport, was enshrined in the Naismith Basketball Hall of Fame in Springfield, Massachusetts, in 1980, six years after he died.

Winning championships at various levels of play helped, but so did his introduction of the weave offense. The five players lined up in a 1-2-2 formation. At Wyoming, Sailors was the "1," the ball handler who jump-started each possession. He passed to a wing, then darted over and tried to spring him free.

"The rule was that every time you passed the ball you set a screen," Sailors said.

If things were clicking, each time a pass was made, the ball was advanced closer to the basket until a player spotted an opening and could shoot. It was that offense that the freshmen began learning and which they gradually mastered.

Sailors may have been the progenitor of the little-known or little-appreciated jump shot when he showed up on campus at Wyoming in 1939, and he may have been destined for athletic stardom, but he had no swelled head, no childhood or youthful history of being complimented for his greatness on the court from an early age. In the 2000s, the top junior high school players in the country are identified and highlighted. Twitter, Facebook, and every other form of computer communication brings attention to prodigies before they are even truly ranked as prodigies.

The casual arrival of Sailors on campus as a freshman portended little, particularly since within a few years he and his teammates became authors of a special chapter in the school's athletic history. As the leader of that bunch Sailors, it can be argued, is one of the most famous Wyoming products shy of Buffalo Bill Cody.

But he had to earn that status and when he showed up to enroll in classes Sailors was just another low-on-the-totem-pole freshman. The athletic scholarship as is currently known did not exist at Wyoming. Sailors had to work for his room and board and he waited tables at the Student Union. Not only did he serve meals during dinnertime, he worked in the cafeteria serving soft drinks and malts when students stopped in for snacks.

"I worked behind the counter some and I served meals and waited on the booths," Sailors said. "I did it all. Sometimes we'd clean up and scrub the floors. We did whatever we needed to do. I worked there all through college. So did Jim Weir. We had all the food we wanted to eat, good food. Anything that was in the place we could have it. And they paid us twenty-five cents an hour. That was my spending money. At the time that wasn't too bad when the going wage for working on a farm was a dollar a day."

Probably 90 percent of present-day major-college basketball recruits would think they had been sold into slavery if they had a college work arrangement like Sailors's.

Sailors did not have his tuition waived, either, at least not freshman year. It was paid by the Laramie Elks Club. After that the university covered his tuition. As a freshman Sailors also commuted from home in Hillsdale and did not stay at a fraternity house or dormitory.

"The only reason I went back and slept at home was my mom didn't like to stay alone," Sailors said. "She worked and she quit fooling around with college kids as boarders. She liked to cook and instead she went and cooked at some sorority houses and finally the ATO fraternity house. She liked the kids and they liked her."

If Sailors wanted to change his living arrangement he did not make a big deal out of it when his mother prevailed and kept suggesting he come home nights. The home front situation did not change while he was in school, either, so he did not alter his plans and through his junior year he commuted to campus from his mother's house.

While working at the Student Union was not especially hard labor, it is a far cry from the prevailing image of current-day college sports stars as being pampered. It would seem to be more difficult to get a puffed-up sense of self when you had to deliver the salad and rolls to your fellow frat brothers at dinnertime.

For the most part, compared to his later fame in Wyoming, as a freshman Sailors was just another guy. The freshman team did blend well together and while the squad did play teams besides its own varsity, games were not easy to schedule. Schools did not want to spend much money on their freshmen teams, and in later years, when freshmen were made eligible for the varsity by the NCAA cost was one of the reasons cited.

"We didn't have much competition," Sailors said "Everybody we played, we beat them badly. They didn't want to come up here to Laramie anyway. Very few liked to come up here to this altitude."

While Denver is well-known as the Mile High City, Laramie is also situated near the Rocky Mountains and was built at 7,220 feet above sea level, quite a bit higher than Denver. That meant that visiting teams that were not used to a high altitude were often left gasping for breath. It was a built-in advantage for the Cowboys.

One coach in particular that Sailors recalled despising his teams' hoops visits to Laramie was Frosty Cox, who guided the Colorado Buffaloes between 1936 and 1950.

"Frosty Cox was a good coach and Colorado had some good teams, but Cox just hated to come to Laramie," Sailors said. "You can't really blame him. I don't remember ever losing to Colorado."

Sailors survived his freshman year as a student, waiter, and basketball player, and moved on to the Wyoming varsity his sophomore year during the winter of 1940–41. The savvy Shelton, as he had planned, was turning things around quickly for the Cowboys. The newcomers were difference makers and Wyoming finished that season 14–6. Sailors won his first letter and averaged 7.3 points a game.

It was the real start of things for the Shelton era at Wyoming and it was the true start of things for the freshmen who had beaten the varsity to herald their coming a year earlier. Although he was older and would not still be wearing a Wyoming uniform by the time the team reached its peak a few years later, one of Sailors's teammates was another Wyoming native whose fame far transcended the state in future years—and indeed could safely be said to eclipse Sailors's, as well, though not for his basketball prowess.

Curt Gowdy was a three-year letterman for the Cowboys who became one of the most popular and accomplished sportscasters in history. Gowdy was born two years before Sailors in Green River, Wyoming. His father worked for the Union Pacific Railroad and Gowdy moved to Cheyenne by the time he was six.

Gowdy was a 5-foot-9 guard for the basketball team and a three-year letter winner for the tennis team before graduating in 1942. While his broadcasting career began auspiciously, handling the radio duties for six-man football in Wyoming, his career arc escalated swiftly. Before the end of the decade he was second banana to the legendary Mel Allen in the New York Yankees' broadcast booth. Gowdy later became the lead announcer for the Boston Red Sox and then latched onto high-profile network jobs. Among his accomplishments— fitting for a Wyoming-bred outdoorsman—was introducing the country to the famed *American Sportsman* television show.

Although Gowdy, who passed away in 2006, was no longer a member of the Wyoming basketball team later in the 1940s when it achieved the pinnacle of its success, and Sailors and he were not particularly close friends, Gowdy was a witness to some of Sailors's earliest college performances when the jump shot was a significant factor in games.

In a 1988 comment, Gowdy, who had viewed many thousands of basketball players, said he believed Sailors was among the best he ever saw on the hardwood.

"He was a great dribbler and very, very quick, like a rattlesnake," Gowdy said. "His quickness was the main thing I remember about him. He was a good shot. He was a spectacular player to watch."

One aspect of his sophomore season that Sailors always remembered was his first trip to New York City. In 1940 the entire state of Wyoming had a population of 250,000. In 1940, New York City had a population of 7.5 million. Sailors marveled at the incredible crush of people, the tall buildings, and the traffic jams, but he was less in awe than he thought he might be.

"I was a country guy, but I handled it alright," he said. "I didn't go clear off my rocker."

The Cowboys, continuously earning goodwill with Madison Square Garden promoter and scheduler Ned Irish, played City College of New York on December 30 (they won 49–43), but were already in town by Christmas.

"We'd make those long trips to the East, to Rochester, Philadelphia, New York City, but we were in New York over the Christmas holidays," Sailors said. "One time most of the guys had gone out on the town somewhere and I asked Shelton if he minded if I went to Times Square. The Garden was at West Forty-Ninth Street and Eighth Avenue then, which is only a short walk to Times Square, and we were staying in the Hotel Paramount nearby. I'd heard so much about it. Shelton said, 'Well, Kenny, you go, but you be careful down there. There are all kinds of people in this big city.' I went down there and spent three or four hours, by myself."

The Paramount Hotel, located on West Forty-Sixth Street, and built in 1928, was a choice location, so close to the old Garden that the players went to the games in their warm-up suits and didn't even shower until they returned to their rooms.

There were lessons to be learned on a solo jaunt to Times Square for a somewhat impressionable lad from Wyoming, even if he was cautious. One of those lessons was how hard-hearted New Yorkers could be. Sailors was surprised to see a man having a seizure right on the sidewalk and being ignored.

"People didn't care," he said. "They were stepping over him. I walked around him, but there wasn't anything a guy could do if he started choking. It was wall-to-wall people, with one person after another hitting you up for money. They can recognize if you aren't a New Yorker, I guess. Shelton had warned me, 'Don't give anything to anybody. Just go your own way. Tell them you don't want to be bothered.' So I did. You couldn't walk down the street without people hitting you and bumping into you. Thousands, millions probably. What an experience for a kid raised on a farm in Wyoming going into Times Square at night. It was a fascinating town. I wouldn't want to live there, but it was interesting."

Madison Square Garden was the hotbed of college basketball and it could be thrilling for a young man to play there. The Cowboys were given instructions about the proceedings for player introductions and by custom Sailors was the first man introduced to the crowd when Wyoming played.

"They told us, 'When we call your name, walk through these doors back there, out of the dressing room, and out into the Garden,'" Sailors said. "There were more than eighteen thousand people there."

One thing that occurred during the contest versus CCNY was Kenny Sailors wowing the hoops knowledgeable New York fans with his jump shot. The comparison is obvious, but nonetheless accurate, that Sailors unveiling the newfangled shot was just like a playwright having his show staged elsewhere and then opening on Broadway. Sailors was definitely in the big-time.

Many years later Sailors received a letter from a fan who was a twelve-year-old at the time and who was blown away by watching his deadeye shooting, the likes of which had never been performed by any other player. In the letter, written decades in the future, the boy talks about how he, along with a half-dozen friends, obtained free tickets from Ned Irish and coming into Manhattan from New Jersey.

"They saw me shoot the jump shot," Sailors said. Also included in the note was how he had inspired them to try taking jump shots themselves and incorporate the shot into their own games. They wrote, "We never did master it. We never did master that jump shot."

Apparently, the jump shot was not yet for everyone, as it would become later.

Sophomore year, ending in the spring of 1941, was a prelude to Sailors's junior year. The 1941–42 school year was dramatic and filled with unknowns, not the least of which stemmed from the fact that the United States was at war. Despite desperate efforts to remain neutral, Americans were dragged into World War II by the bombing of Pearl Harbor on December 7, 1941.

While many American men immediately enlisted, leaving behind their jobs and families, their college studies and athletic careers, not every university student was promptly drafted. But as the war spread and the country's commitment to fighting the Nazis in Europe and the Japanese in the Pacific expanded, it was apparent that many more fighting men would be needed and that soon enough all able-bodied potential soldiers would be joining one branch of the military or the other.

Although he could not know what lay ahead in his immediate future, when Sailors returned to school in the autumn of 1941 he could sense that big changes loomed. That year the Cowboys finished 15–5—they were making inroads against their competition, developing cohesiveness playing together, and each player was improving. The players stuck together, learned together, and played better than ever together, yet were sometimes distracted by world events. As it so happened, the team remained together throughout the season and moved on together for the 1942–43 campaign, the scheduled senior year for Sailors and the other freshmen who entered Wyoming together in September of 1939.

The school year of 1942–43, and the year 1943 in particular, was the single most monumental year in Sailors's life, not only as an athlete, but off the court as well.

In September, when the school year began, Sailors did not have a girlfriend. Before the end of the next summer, he was married. When the basketball season began Sailors was a known commodity in Wyoming. By the end of March he was nationally celebrated. Before the end of 1943 he was not merely a warrior on the basketball court, but a warrior wearing another kind of uniform representing the United States in the greatest and most horrific conflict ever known, with the largest death toll of 60 million recorded in a single war.

CHAPTER 4

A Special Someone and a Special Season

KENNY MET MARILYNNE IN THE FALL OF 1942, introduced by a friend at the University of Wyoming who later became governor of the state.

Sailors's friend Stan Hathaway, in the future Wyoming's twenty-seventh governor, worked at the Kappa House, home to a woman's sorority, and that seemed like a more pleasing arrangement for a college-aged single guy than what Sailors was doing. At the time Sailors was waiting his tables at the Student Union, Hathaway's job was to clean the Kappa House, vacuum, dust, wash dishes, and sometimes serve at the dinner table—but clientele consisted almost only of eligible young ladies. Hathaway used to tease Sailors that he wasn't meeting the right girls and that he should be waiting on tables at Kappa House, not the Student Union.

"You sure are missing out on things," Hathaway told Sailors, upon informing him that he was surrounded by all of these college girls that he got to know at the dormitory.

"Are you keeping them all for yourself?" Sailors retorted.

No, he wasn't, Hathaway said, he would be glad to share. One day after this exchange, Hathaway, who later in life would prove to have a winning enough personality to attract men and women to his side when he sought elective office, showed up on Sailors's doorstep at the union with four young women in tow, all of them from the same Wyoming home city of Casper, and they all sat in one booth.

Although a junior, between basketball, class work, and work, Sailors had not been active dating anyone and he had been joking when he suggested

Hathaway was trying to corner the market on all of the pretty young women on the campus. Hathaway even sensed that the prettiest girl in the group was the one for Sailors and singled out Marilynne for extra praise. His instincts were correct.

"They were all pretty nice-looking girls, but of course I thought the woman who became my wife was the prettiest," Sailors said.

Hathaway was kind enough to make introductions and to Sailors he said, "Kenny, these are the beautiful girls from Casper I was telling you about." Then he added, "This is Marilynne. I was telling you about her."

Truth be told, Marilynne wasn't a complete stranger to Sailors. Not that he knew her or had ever spoken to her, but he had seen her stop in at the Student Union occasionally to drink a Coca-Cola with friends. Sailors had been struck by her appeal, but had never ingratiated himself with her.

Bringing Marilynne and the girls over was only a preliminary step in Hathaway's matchmaking. He said, "Isn't your fraternity dance this weekend, Kenny?" Sailors said it was, but that he didn't dance. Undeterred, Hathaway said, "Marilynne, you told me you don't dance a whole lot, that you didn't care for it."

Still, Kenny was closemouthed. Hathaway was the one carrying the ball to the goal line. He basically asked Marilynne to go to the frat dance with Kenny and she accepted, without Sailors doing a bit of the work. "Well, sure, I'd to go his fraternity dance with him."

"That was our first date," Sailors said. "We didn't dance. We just talked. Later, she taught me a little, enough for me to get by on the dance floor. We had fun. We hit it right off. I learned that she liked to hunt and fish. Later on, we went fishing on a lot of our dates."

Marilynne was an attractive and feisty blonde who was athletic. She had played high school basketball, such as it was for secondary school girls in the 1930s and 1940s long before the more polished women's game took hold. Kenny and Marilynne, whom Sailors later almost always referred to by her nickname of Bokie, began dating.

The young ballplayer didn't have much money and many times the "dates" consisted of the couple sitting around Bokie's sorority house just talking, or taking fishing trips to nearby creeks and streams. The nearby Snowy Range was home to many bountiful bodies of water, but Marilynne was not the type to bat her eyelashes, pretend she didn't know what she was doing, and ask her date for help baiting a hook. She definitely knew what to do with a rod and reel and when they set up by those creeks they fished hard.

"We competed to see who could catch the most fish," Sailors said. "We always competed with each other."

Now that's one way to a man's heart, especially if he never let ego get in the way when challenged. They also took hikes on the outskirts of town in the hills, something Bokie initiated. They'd picnic on the trip.

"When we could find someone to let us use some horses, we'd go riding," Sailors said. "Marilynne liked all of that outdoors stuff. At first I thought she was just kidding me, but she really liked all of it. When I began to realize it, we really hit it off."

Kenny being a basketball player was a bonus for Bokie, who died in 2002. "She was a player," Sailors said. "She loved it. She was a good athlete. She became a cheerleader."

The Wyoming basketball team provided a lot for cheerleaders and fans alike to root for during the 1942–43 season that remains the finest in school history, and so did her boyfriend, who was about to produce just about the finest all-around player season in school history, too.

Kenny and Marilynne did click from the start and began spending most of their free time together. Within a few months Kenny asked her to marry him and early in the new calendar year they became engaged.

As if attending the same school and having basketball in common wasn't enough, Marilynne also grew up with a fairly rural background and learned to shoot at an early age.

"Bokie was like my mother in that she grew up with a gun," Sailors said. "My mom was a good shot. Remember, she could take that gun and go out and shoot the head of a chicken off. That's how good she was."

When they met, Bokie was a freshman, and she possessed the same shooting skills Sailors's mother did. Hanging around with either one, Sailors would never starve. Whatever meat he couldn't put on the table, his wife or mother would. They were also both down-to-earth and commonsense people.

"Those two women in my life, my wife and my mother, had more influence on me in my whole life than any other two people," Sailors said.

Even if Hathaway, who was governor between 1967 and 1975 and passed away in 2005, didn't think much of Sailors's job at the Student Union, it had at least one more advantage. At one time or another every student on campus passed through, and combined with Sailors's burgeoning fame on the basketball court, his role at the Union made him familiar to everyone, too.

Whether it was hitting jump shots or busing tables that served as the more effective campaign platform, everyone knew Kenny Sailors and he won the Most Popular Student award three times at Wyoming. Once the 1942–43 college basketball season began, it was a safe bet that basketball contributed more to Sailors's renown than working the Union dining room, and that numerous non-eligible voters in the community recognized his name, too.

The most glorious ride in Wyoming college basketball history began on December 11, 1942, with a 49–33 defeat of Fort Warren. It was a busy day because the Cowboys played a doubleheader against Fort Warren, winning a second time, 53–43, as well. This was a preseason road trip to Georges Island in Massachusetts where the fort was named for Dr. James Warren, a casualty of the Battle of Bunker Hill during the Revolutionary War. The fort inhabits the entrance to Boston Harbor. A week later Wyoming also defeated the Fort Warren All-Stars, 63–40. In the big picture these games were inconsequential, but they did allow Coach Everett Shelton to see what he had on his roster when his guys were placed under pressure that would not be present during an intra-squad scrimmage.

Shelton was a veteran coach and although he was the head man at Wyoming (the only statewide school in a state with a tiny population), his aspirations were grander than his surroundings. He left AAU coaching to win a national title in college ball, but no matter how much talent he had he knew that he had to show it off in the right places for publicity and to him that meant touring the northeastern section of the country. In those days basketball was far more important in the big cities of the East than it was in any other region of the country. Basketball mattered most in Boston, Philadelphia, New York, and the Atlantic states.

Once the touring Cowboys polished off Fort Warren the season began for real with a contest at Duquesne in Pittsburgh. Wyoming lost, 43–33, and that shook up Shelton and the team, made them wonder if they were really all that good. Although in recent years the Dukes have not made a splash on the NCAA scene, during the 1920s, 1930s, and 1940s, Duquesne fielded several powerhouse clubs.

Charles "Chick" Davis took the reins of the program for the 1924–25 season. By 1942–43 he was established as a winner. Davis missed a couple of years at the helm during World War II, but concluded his service at Duquesne with

314 victories and a near-75 percent winning average. A loss to Duquesne was nothing to be ashamed of, but it was sobering.

Clearly, the Cowboys learned from their defeat. They did not lose again on their journey East and did not lose again for a long, long time. Wyoming bested Albright College, 56–52, in Reading, Pennsylvania, LaSalle, 56–32, in Philadelphia, St. Francis of Pennsylvania, 63–38 at Madison Square Garden in New York, Rochester, 68–44, in upstate New York, and Lawrence Tech, 78–34, in Southfield, Michigan. So the Cowboys were 8–1 before abandoning the Eastern time zone and boarding a train just after the New Year's holiday.

Most of the opponents were not regarded highly nationally, but St. Francis was 6–0 when the Terriers met Wyoming and although there really was no home team the crowd at the country's mecca of basketball bought 13,240 tickets for what became a New York City institution at the site—the college hoops doubleheader.

Ned Irish, the showman and entrepreneur who later owned the New York Knickerbockers when they played in the early days of the NBA, was the foremost early promoter of college basketball. He scoured the nation looking for attractive teams and he didn't care if your school was located two thousand miles west of the Garden. If he thought you could play and would put on a good show you got an invite. Wyoming filled that role and Shelton worked Irish for invitations to their mutual benefit.

Wyoming manhandled St. Francis, a 25-point margin of victory making a very public statement for western basketball's quality. Most of the Cowboys scoring that day came from three players. Sailors, who had been chosen as captain of the team, notched 18 points, forward Jim Weir scored 17 points, and center Milo Komenich scored 21 points.

Komenich was from Gary, Indiana, and he stood 6-foot-7. He was the missing link in the lineup for the Cowboys, the big man in the middle needed to contend with other teams' strong men, and a sweeper on the glass who provided the rebounds to jump-start Wyoming's increasingly impressive and important fast break on offense.

His recruitment, if that is the right word during those dark ages of high school recruiting, was a coup for Shelton. Komenich had already graduated from high school and was playing AAU ball.

"Milo had been out of school for a few years," Sailors said. "He was older. Shelton found him and brought him to Wyoming."

Indeed, Komenich, who would later play several years of professional ball after his All-American career at Wyoming, was already twenty when he showed up in Laramie. Blending holdover players, Sailors's freshman group, and some new players, Wyoming had every piece it needed to compete well under the bright lights that Shelton never shied from. The others who got into the game against St. Francis, and who played varying roles during the season, included Floyd Volker, Lew Roney, Earl "Shadow" Ray, who was at heart a football player first, Jim Collins, Jim Reese, and Don Waite.

The newspapers, such as the hometown *Laramie Boomerang*, the *Wyoming Eagle* in Cheyenne, and the bigger Denver papers located roughly 125 miles to the south, did not send sportswriters on the road to report on Cowboys games—too expensive for them. Typically, they either used wire service reports or put together a handful of paragraphs on their own through use of the telephone.

A story about the Wyoming–St. Francis contest noted that New York University was at that moment the only undefeated major college team with a 7–0 record. The Wyoming game, it stated, was "close only for the first few minutes, but the Cowboys took the lead at the eight-minute mark and were never headed."

Yet the big-city newspapers of New York and the East were meeting Sailors and Komenich for the first time and their writers were impressed. Sailors was a revelation to them when Wyoming dumped St. Francis.

"Wyoming height controlled the airlanes and Kenny Sailors' stutter-dribble took care of the ground attack in a one-man blitzkrieg," wrote the reporter on the scene from the *New York Times*, who employed war metaphors because World War II was raging overseas. "This Sailors, already being boomed for All-America, shakes off defensive men like Rommel outrunning Il Duce's dupes on the Tripoli Highway," the story read.

Perhaps Rochester did not rate major-college status, but the school did have a good team despite incurring a 22-point trouncing from Wyoming. A Rochester-based reporter commented on Sailors's prowess leading up to that game, writing, "Ken Sailors . . . is one of the speediest and classiest dribblers in the business."

In its report about the contest, the Associated Press said the Cowboys were "snapping the University of Rochester's twenty-two-game winning streak." Komenich scored 30 points for Wyoming. Also, "Eighteen of the Cowboy points were credited to Captain Kenny Sailors, who played brilliant ball for thirty-nine minutes."

The brief report from the LaSalle game had nearly as many words in a subhead as in the story, but the point was made that five thousand people attended the game versus Wyoming at Convention Hall and that Komenich and Sailors were too much for the hosts to handle defensively. Sailors led the Cowboys with 20 points and Komenich contributed 14. The story referred to Komenich and Sailors as being "rated the best shooting forwards in (their) part of the country." Neither Komenich, the center, nor Sailors, a guard, played forward.

Historically, Wyoming and Utah have engaged in spirited, close games. Not in early 1943 when the Cowboys demolished Utah twice in Salt Lake City. The combined talents of Mr. Outside, Sailors, and Mr. Inside, Komenich, was proving unstoppable for most defenses.

"It is impossible that both Sailors and Komenich will be lassoed in the same game," wrote the *Rocky Mountain News*.

Still playing on the road, Wyoming resumed its schedule on January 15 at Utah with a 66–38 thumping of the Utes and a follow-up ravaging of the Utes the next day, by a 68–26 margin that meant that it was difficult in good conscience to obtain too much playing time for the starters. On January 22, the Cowboys handled Colorado State, 66–42, in Fort Collins.

Although the school athletic teams are uniformly called Utes now, they were generally called the Redskins at the time. They were also referred to in print at times as the Indians.Whatever the preferred nickname, Utah offered no challenge to Wyoming and admiration for the Cowboys was apparent in the writing from the *Deseret News* correspondent on the scene. The lead on the paper's story about the 42-point defeat absorbed by Utah, read this way: "Wyoming's brilliant basketball crew, which has averaged close to 60 points per game this season fattened its shooting average Saturday night by handing the University of Utah Redskins one of their worst lickings in years, 68–26, before another big crowd of about three thousand fans. . . ."

Some other high points of the story penned by assistant sports editor Jimmy Hodgson showered compliments on Wyoming. He cited a "sensational shooting exhibition" from Komenich, who scored 26 points. And, "Ken Sailors showed all his usual flash with the leather and dribbled all around the Indians . . ."

Hodgson concluded that this was a very special visiting team. "The victory also left little doubt that Coach Ev Shelton has one of the classiest basketball crews that has ever been produced in this region," Hodgson wrote.

"What has occurred is that the Wyoming Cowboys under Everett Shelton's mentoring have jelled. The Cowboys may have a once-in-a-lifetime team at a once-in-a-lifetime moment. The combination of leadership, ability, and opportunity meshed, and the team is ripe for the situation, prepared to seize this moment and exploit it."

Shelton was inclined to be tough on his players. Sailors attributed it to the coach's military background as a Marine.

"Tougher than a boot, that old boy was," Sailors said. "I suppose he was about my size as far as height goes, but he was all man in every respect. He wouldn't hesitate a minute to grab some big, 6-foot-8 player and jerk him around like he was a rag doll. If he needed to do it, he would. He was a tough coach, but he was a nice guy as long as you didn't do things that you knew you shouldn't do. If so, you had no problem with him. He laid down the rules. Yes, we had a curfew. You bet. You didn't mess with the rules if you wanted to play ball for him."

There were rules about what to eat, rules about lights out, and rules against drinking.

"The whole works," Sailors said. "Most of us wanted to win and wanted to play badly enough that we didn't break any rules. I never did. Coaches back in those days were tough compared to the ones today. There's no comparison. Players knew if they broke the rules, they were gone. If you drank one beer, you're gone, thrown off the team for the season."

Discipline came with the playbook if you wanted to play for Everett Shelton. He was strict, but he also won everywhere he coached. That was his method.

"Every kid is tempted, you know," Sailors said. "Your best friends sometimes are the ones that try to get you to smoke a little pot, you know, 'to relax.' Sometimes other players would say to me, 'Sailors, have a little fun once in a while. Aw, come on, drink a couple of beers with us.' I hated beer. I'd say, 'I don't like it. Don't push beer off on me. And I don't bother with whiskey or any of that stuff.' Your best friends will try to get you involved if they're doing it. I don't know why that is, but they always do."

From his military haircut to his erect bearing, from his early-to-bed, early-to-rise regimen, there is no doubt that Sailors then, and now, was always a straight arrow. He was a very dedicated athlete. He had been a skinny little kid when he began playing basketball and through lessons learned going up against his big brother he knew that size and strength could be a great advantage on the court. He couldn't do anything about his height, but he could get stronger. That was long before athletes lifted weights to build bulk. But

Sailors worked summers, shifts that were ten hours long, hauling hundred-pound bags of cement onto freight cars. That was just like pumping iron in terms of results. He also spent extra time not only shooting the jumpers, but honing his dribbling skills, something that was overshadowed by the jump shot, but was just as important to his all-around game. Sailors spent hours doing dexterity drills such as dribbling in and out of a row of chairs placed on the court.

Beginning with his playing days at Wyoming Sailors has watched college basketball for decades, as it has mushroomed in popularity through phenomenally unbelievable television exposure being shown more often than *Law and Order*, and he has watched all of the great college coaches draw up Xs and Os. He contrasted Shelton's comparatively low-key bench style to some of the animated coaches of present-day college ball, who patrol the sidelines like big cats in a cage at the zoo and shout directions on every offensive possession with laryngitis-inducing loudness.

"Shelton was very quiet during games," Sailors said. "He sat on the bench. Very seldom did he get up and walk around like these coaches do. None of that. He sat right there. He did his coaching in practice. He didn't try to do it during the games so much like these crazy coaches today. They try to coach too much during the game. All they do is confuse their athletes. Maybe they can call out a play or something, but the rest of the time a lot of it is nonsense. Kids don't pay attention to them. They go right out and do what they want to do."

Shelton drilled his men hard in practice, drumming into them the basics of the "Shelton Weave." He expected them to absorb his lessons through repetition and the learning curve was supposed to end at the locker room door. By the time the games started the players were supposed to know the offense's intricacies and what they were supposed to do when the jump ball took place. During games it was all about execution to Shelton. His boys had the tools and now it was time to use them to win.

What began as the Shelton Weave in the 1930s is no longer called that. Whether it is the T formation in football, or zone defensive traps, innovations enter a sport and once employed with success, they are fair game for copying, and even for tinkering with to make them more effective. The offense in vogue today is the "motion" offense, but Sailors swears allegiance to the weave.

"It's just a great offense," Sailors said. "If young coaches want to use it they can open the middle up so their center doesn't have to fool with three or four

Teams did not take videos of their games, never mind trade game films with opposing teams. Only word of mouth worked against the play fooling teams forever, and the occasional photograph.

"Everybody got to know that we were so good at it," Sailors said, "so teams started putting a man back. We scored I don't know how many baskets doing that for a couple of years."

Komenich had his role defined fairly precisely by Shelton from the moment that he stepped off the train from the Midwest. Shelton took Komenich aside, put his arm around him and explained the facts of life. Not the birds and the bees, but the Xs and Os and where he fit into the Wyoming scheme.

"You see this line that goes down here," Shelton said, pointing to the free-throw circle. Komenich replied that he did indeed see the line. "That circle that goes around, don't bother with anything that is happening outside of it. It doesn't belong to you. But anything that goes on inside that line, from there to the basket, is yours. Anybody that comes in there, throw them out." And as Sailors said with a smile, "That's exactly what Milo did. He was the best down there."

Once in a great while Komenich defied the parameters of his job. He was a left-handed shooter who could make a long-distance set shot from what would be today's three-point range, and periodically he felt the need to prove it.

"He was a threat," Sailors said. "He didn't shoot from outside much, but he could. They had to cover him. You didn't dare lay off him. That's why sometimes we put him in the corner. Jim Weir was a great outside shooter, too, and Weir could drive. They complemented each other in the front court."

After one of history's longest road trips through the East and in Utah and at Colorado State, the Cowboys finally had a home game on January 23, 1943, a rematch against Colorado State. The Cowboys romped, 49–23, a defensive performance so stingy that Scrooge would be jealous. Playing in front of the mob of happy fans at home was energizing, too.

The Cowboys' arena was called the Half Acre Gym. Although the home schedule was light that season, nobody could touch Wyoming there. The Cowboys were unbeaten at home during the 1942–43 season and were rarely even pressed. The worst drubbing delivered was to Regis of Denver on January 28 when Wyoming annihilated the visitors, 101–45.

For the era, that was a completely outlandish score. College basketball teams did not break 100 points in games. They did not top 90 or even 80, except on very rare days. A few weeks later an Associated Press story out of New York examining the high-scoring teams of the year noted that Wyoming was tied for being the third-highest scoring club in the nation with 61.6 points a game. College basketball was a much slower-paced game at the time and if one of the best teams in the land was only scoring at that clip, their 56-point win over Regis was stunning.

Shelton was enthusiastic about showing off his team in major cities far from his Skyline Conference games, and had no qualms about the disproportionate number of home and away games his squad played. The normal process in the 2000s is to stack the pre-conference game schedule with home dates against less-capable opponents. Shelton had an "anytime, anywhere" philosophy for taking on challenges and wanted to showcase the Cowboys against the best available teams when he could.

Besides, except for league foes, most teams did not want to journey to Laramie. Sailors said the home gym was so intimidating for visiting teams that it was nicknamed "Hell's Half Acre." For those teams passing through it was like stepping into a furnace with the heat turned up all the way when they had to face the good Wyoming ball clubs.

Nonconference scheduling was brutal for Wyoming. Teams refused Shelton's offers of home-and-home series.

"They wouldn't come here," Sailors said. "They always said, 'No, we won't come to Laramie. It's too high up there.' Shelton would say, 'OK, we'll play you twice on your court, but we need the finances, so we'll take the gate money from one game. And they always agreed to it. He said, 'You pay the expenses, and give the rest to us.'"

Home or away, East or West, except for the stumble against Duquesne, the Cowboys were turning Shelton into a prophet. They won and they won some more—and everywhere, since they had just nine home games all season. At the beginning of February, Wyoming journeyed to Oklahoma to take on Phillips 66, the always-rugged AAU club, for two games. The games were played for charity, to benefit polio research. This was intense competition against older players, some of whom had been collegiate All-Americans themselves. Wyoming won the first game, 42–41, in overtime, and took the second game, 37–36.

Trimming Phillips 66 twice, on its own court yet, was a tremendous achievement, and drew even more attention to Wyoming as a growing powerhouse. A reporter summing up the two games called Wyoming the "greatest college basketball team in the nation." The crowd witnessing what was considered an upset totaled sixty-five hundred the second night. The game was broadcast on the radio and the announcers made pleas for the charity during the action. The initial estimate was that more than $10,000 was raised for the cause by the two encounters. It was said that stations all over the broadcast region were receiving donations of nickels, dimes, and quarters, even from those who could least afford to give.

Both games were close calls for the Cowboys against a very worthy opponent. Once more the accounts of the games highlighted play by Komenich and Sailors. "Coach Everett Shelton's classy aggregation carved Wednesday night's glorious triumph (the 37–36 game) out of the uncanny clutch shooting of Milo Komenich, the flawless all-around play of Kenny Sailors and a cruel twist of fate . . .," it was reported. The fate comment referred to a first-half Phillips shot that went in at the buzzer, but was disallowed for being a split second late.

Sailors scored 14 points and Komenich 12 in the low-scoring showdown. In setting up a daunting schedule and in not giving a fig where his team competed, Shelton demonstrated ultimate confidence in the Cowboys. They gained experience and were hardened by playing the best in trying, on-the-road circumstances.

Later, a somewhat-awestruck questioner asked Shelton if he would be willing to play against China since his team bested everyone else. China was not exactly known as a world basketball power at the time and, with World War II unleashed and the Japanese roaming over its shores, was not really in a position to play anybody in any sport, so it certainly was an offbeat question. Yet Shelton answered the query with all seriousness. "I'll play China," Shelton said, "but they've got to come here. We're not going to go all of the way over there. If they want to come here, tell them we'll play them at a neutral court at Madison Square Garden."

By then Shelton viewed the palace of college basketball as almost as cozy a home as Hell's Half Acre. His guys might have been country boys, but they adapted well to the huge metropolis. He did a selling job on the Cowboys, letting them know how important it was for them to gain recognition and a reputation in the big city, which was not routinely being called the Big Apple quite yet, although the name had been used casually in some earlier twentieth-century references.

As early as their freshmen seasons, Shelton told his incoming players that they should get used to trips to New York.

"He sat us down with the varsity," Sailors said, "and he said, 'Boys, look, all the publicity in the game of basketball comes out of New York City. The primary place for a college team to play, if it wants publicity, and it wants to play great teams, is in Madison Square Garden. I know Ned Irish, the general manager of Madison Square Garden.'"

As part of his pep talks Shelton explained that when he came to Wyoming he came with a goal. In the pre-organized professional league days of the 1930s, when there was not yet an NBA, AAU ball was the best around. He told his Cowboys, "Boys, I've won championships at the highest level of basketball. That's AAU. When you win a national championship, you're beating the best athletes in the country. I've won championships there and now I want to win a college championship. That's my desire. You Wyoming kids, you've got more than I thought you'd have. I think we can do it."

Shelton knew, however, that he would have to convince the rest of the college basketball world that Wyoming was the real deal and Irish proved to be an invaluable ally in getting the message out. Shelton loved Broadway and Irish loved the Cowboys. He made Wyoming teams feel welcome and he gave them that forum for publicity.

"He really took care of us," Sailors said of the nine players who were on the traveling team. "He'd meet us when we came to town. We'd board the train in Laramie and go overnight into Denver and then on to Chicago. Then we'd switch to the New York Central and come into Grand Central Station. Ned Irish would meet us when we were stepping off the train. Shelton introduced all of us to him and he called him the greatest basketball promoter who ever lived. And he was, just about."

The players liked Irish, and why wouldn't they? He made them feel welcome in the alien big city of New York and gave them tickets to Broadway shows.

"We'd see the big musicals with tickets he gave us," Sailors said. "Personally, I'd rather have somebody sing cowboy songs, but when we walked into the theaters as a team everybody looked at us. He gave us anything we wanted. We went to see the Rockettes, too. We visited some very classy places where the men were dressed in tuxedos and the women wore high heels and long dresses. We just wanted to see what it was all about."

After the attention-getting Phillips 66 series, the Cowboys hung around Laramie for the month of February. They built up exactly no frequent train miles on the Union Pacific, the New York Central, or any other railroad line that month, but they did take on Utah twice more, this time at the Half Acre, and posted victories of 75–46 and 45–31.

The next victims up on campus were the Brigham Young University Cougars, also from Utah. Up until then Wyoming had earned itself some national exposure, but hadn't really won anything. The trio of BYU games represented a series to name the Skyline Conference champion. A meaningful trophy was at stake.

CHAPTER 5

Conference Champs and NCAA Bound

WYOMING BECAME ONE OF THE MOST DOMINANT TEAMS in the land during the 1942–43 season, but the stakes increased as the year wore on. When the Brigham Young University Cougars traveled to Laramie in late February it was up to the Cowboys to prove that they were the best team in their league, the Skyline Conference, which was also referred to as the Big Seven, or sometimes the Mountain States Conference, during those years.

The Cowboys loomed as the favorite before the three-game season and only part of it was because they were the home club. Wyoming had more height than BYU and was a more seasoned team thanks to Coach Everett Shelton's touring ways that threw the players into a variety of situations that hardened them. It was understood that the winner of the series would have the inside track for a berth in the NCAA playoffs.

By the time BYU arrived at the Half Acre, the Cowboys had been undefeated since December and had won seventeen games in a row. Wyoming's record was 20–1, with the only loss—the one to Duquesne—growing dimmer in the rearview mirror.

Also, before the teams met, the Skyline Conference all-league team had been announced. Wyoming's honorees were Kenny Sailors, Milo Komenich, and Jim Weir. Brigham Young forward Brady Walker was also cited.

The first contest in the series gave Wyoming its eighteenth straight triumph by a 53–42 margin. The Cowboys led pretty much all of the way after opening with a 10–5 start. It was 29–17 Wyoming at halftime.

BYU's strategy was to swarm Komenich in the low post and prevent him

Taken during a Cowboys–Brigham Young University game in February 1943, this is believed to be the earliest photographic evidence of Kenny's jump shot. (Photo courtesy the University of Wyoming.)

from getting open shots. Komenich scored 15 points anyway, but the key to Wyoming's win was how the offense adapted. With Komenich surrounded, opportunities for Sailors abounded, either on drives to the hoop or to use his stop and pop jump shot. Sailors was high man in the game with 21 points. Sailors and Weir consistently beat the Cougars' defense down-court for fast-break buckets that were initiated by Komenich's board work.

Determined not to be burned by Wyoming's speed the next night Brigham Young tried to control the pace and slow it down considerably. The maneuver did change the tempo of the game and kept it close, but Wyoming prevailed in the end, 47–43. A third contest was no-contest with Wyoming finishing off the Cougars a third straight game, 66–43. BYU simply could no longer hang with the Cowboys.

In the finale Sailors scored 28 points and Komenich added 16. Another all-conference team, this one supervised by the *Denver Post*, was announced following the championships. Sailors, Komenich, and Weir were all selected first-team. In Komenich and Weir Wyoming had two of the three best big men in the league. However, Weir was sensitive to the fact that he had been moved out of the center position to the forward wing. Part of that was due to Weir's versatility. Also, Komenich could play one position, and one position only, and that was in the middle. Weir was fast enough to play forward, as well as being large enough to spend time at center.

"You don't find big men that are as quick and fast as he was," Sailors said. "He could have played point guard. He was that good."

Weir resented not playing the center spot and it was obvious to insiders that there was some tension between Weir and Komenich.

"I was the captain and Shelton came to me and said, 'Kenny, you can see there's a little friction between Milo and Jim,'" Sailors said. "Shelton said we were lucky that it didn't show up on the floor, but he was worried about it. I had to admit I had known about it for a couple of years. Shelton said, 'Kenny, we need both of those guys in the game at the same time. We can't put Komenich anywhere but on the inside. He can't play forward. He's not fast enough. Weir can play anywhere. You talk to Jim.'"

Sailors and Weir roomed together on the road and Sailors took advantage of those away-from-the-court moments to both build up Weir's ego and explain how important it was to the welfare of the team for him to get along with Komenich.

"Weir realized that we had to have him and Komenich in the game at the same time when we played good teams," Sailors said. "Once Weir got it through his head we were OK. Komenich was always easygoing and eventually they ended up rooming together."

Although the lineup was usually announced as including a center, two forwards, and two guards, in reality the Cowboys were running a 1-3-1 offense and Sailors was the only guard. He was not only the playmaker, but a scorer. As a rule point guards are seen as the coach on the floor, or as an extension of the head coach on the court. In Wyoming's case that was certainly true. Shelton put huge responsibility on Sailors's shoulder and trusted him implicitly.

"Shelton told me, 'I want you to run everything,'" Sailors said. "'I'm not going to call time out. You decide if the situation is right for Komenich.' Then he told Komenich, 'Sailors is calling the shots.' He knew that I knew the game well enough, in some ways as well as him. He was such a great coach."

The *Denver Post*'s story accompanying the all-league announcement gushed about Sailors, although it referred to him as a forward instead of a guard. "Sailors' all-around play was by far the best in the circuit," the non-bylined piece read, "earning him a spot close to the all-time great forwards of regional basketball."

Sailors was ahead of his time with the jump shot, but he was more than just an outside shooter with a tricky approach. He brought a perfect balance between shooting from outside, whether it was six feet from the basket, or thirty feet from the basket, and his dazzling dribbling that enabled him to get the quick first step to the hoop for layups.

"Your outside shot is no good if you can't drive the ball," Sailors said. "They'll just get up in your face. A good defensive man will just get right up and keep you from shooting the outside shot. And if they know all you can do is drive, they'll stop you. You've got to have them both because one influences the other. That's where I came in. Most of the time I took the jump shot at the top of the key—about twenty feet out.

Sailors made his reputation in the Rocky Mountain region and it was one that was never forgotten. Even decades later his moves and his shot were well remembered and noted when talk turned to area hoops history.

Once the Brigham Young series was completed, with the three victories in the books, it was mostly a situation of staying busy for the Cowboys as they awaited a call from the new NCAA tournament played since 1939 to crown a national champion. Wyoming bested Howard-Payne, Colorado Mines, Poudre Valley, and the Denver American Legion team.

Interestingly, the Denver Legion team, populated with men older than college age, was not a simple tune-up. The Cowboys lost, 41–33, for only the second time all season, in the national AAU tournament. It was a bit of a surprise that the Skyline Conference allowed Wyoming to compete because in prior years it had turned down such requests from its members. However, this year, with World War II raging, all proceeds from the event were to benefit servicemen.

The college boys were outplayed, although Sailors shined once more and was named "Most Promising Youngster." He was the only college player selected for the AAU All-American team in 1943. Denver had two of the first five.

"I have to be honest, but the guy they put on me was probably one of the fastest players who ever tried to cover me," Sailors said. "I could still get away from him most of the time, but he was a former football player and he knocked me around quite a bit. It was intentional. I understand now why he did it, but

In a game against Denver University at Half Acre Gym on February 15, 1946, Kenny takes his signature jump shot. (Photo courtesy the University of Wyoming.)

when I was younger I didn't. He kept talking to me, too, saying, 'Sailors, just leave your feet once and that's the last time you'll shoot a jump shot against anybody.' He kept saying that. I thought maybe the guy was crazy enough to do it. He really psyched me out.

"I only scored 8 or 9 points. Shelton told me not to talk about how I was covered because people would think I was a crybaby since we lost.

The game could be described as a head-straightener, meaning that if the players were in danger of getting swelled heads and puffed-up egos, this result brought them back to earth. Wyoming followed the loss with a 58–45 win over Denver University.

Wyoming was 27–2 on the season. The Cowboys fulfilled Shelton's confidence in them and grew in confidence as a team as the wins piled up and the months passed.

"Coach was behind all of that," Sailors said. "He didn't start by telling us we were the best. He showed us we were good, but stressed that we still had a few things to learn about his offense."

The Duquesne loss came as a surprise and the Cowboys had to overcome the doubt it placed in their minds.

"Shelton began telling us, 'Look boys, we're doing alright,'" Sailors said. "I never talk about that game [the loss]. Shelton said it wouldn't do any good to be crying because you got beat. He said, 'Don't even talk about it.'"

When the team arrived in Pittsburgh Shelton was informed that the game was being moved out of the big arena and into a small recreational facility with a cage around the court. The reason, he was told, was that heavy rains had damaged the court. In the early days of the sport players were sometimes called cagers because of those types of courts. The court was also very small. The combination of Duquesne's zone defense and the smaller court took away Wyoming's offensive game.

"It was a little box," Sailors said. "If you took one step beyond the court you hit the wall. We never practiced against a zone defense, but Shelton said to just move the ball faster and make a faster shift. On a big court that's true, but if you're playing in a little band box like that the zone is the best defense. Shelton never booked Duquesne again."

Shelton wasn't afraid to take his team on the road, but when they were home at the Half Acre, the Cowboys were nearly untouchable. And because Wyoming traveled so much the home fans made sure to turn out in force. Typically, the Cowboys played to overflow crowds, and sometimes games were even piped into the Student Union on the radio to handle fans that were turned away at the gate. The only thing Shelton asked was for school officials not to set up chairs under the baskets. He didn't want to cramp Sailors's style (or his other players') on their drives. If students wanted to hang from the rafters or stand in the balcony that was OK and quarters were tight.

Although Sailors was a top scorer, averaging 15 points a game that season, he gained more satisfaction, and remembered best, his give-and-take with Komenich, who averaged 16.7 points a game that year.

"I didn't worry about trying to be the top scorer," Sailors said. "Milo was the top scorer. I threw him the ball and he probably scored 90 percent of the time. If you got him the ball, especially with that left hand, boy, he was tough. I'd watch his man. I'd dribble left out front, fake, and the guy would jump around to that side, and I'd fake him again. He'd jump back and I'd fake him over there. I'd get him off to the side and Milo had perfect position. I'd take about three real quick steps to the baseline and hit him with a bounce pass. He was moving already and he just laid it up. We worked together and I don't know how many times we did that. He knew me and I knew him."

The four-year-old NCAA tournament of 1943 was only a toddler in age. It was far from the grandiose spectacle that it is in the 2000s, when every game is nationally televised, the profits distributed to colleges and conferences reach into the millions, and it is figured that more than a billion dollars is wagered on game results.

Yet the tournament was on its way, and it carried the prestige of crowning an official national college championship team. The tournament opened with quarterfinal games being played in the East and West regions. The East regional was at Madison Square Garden in New York and the West regional was held in Municipal Auditorium in Kansas City, Missouri.

The eastern teams were Dartmouth, DePaul, Georgetown, and New York University. The four western teams were Oklahoma, Texas, Washington, and Wyoming. These days sixty-eight teams are invited to the tournament.

These days it takes six playoff wins to capture the title. In 1943 it took just three. These days it takes three weeks to determine a champion. In 1943 it took only a handful of days. Many of the games today are played in football stadiums. In 1943, a venue such as Madison Square Garden with a capacity of around twenty thousand was enormous.

Wyoming had the talent and the depth to play with anyone. Of that the Cowboys were certain. They had grown closer, too. Komenich, later an insurance salesman who sold more than a million dollars in policies, and Weir, who was wounded by shrapnel during World War II, had become buddies.

The backups understood their roles and were solid contributors. Shadow Ray spelled Sailors at guard once in a while, and he had excellent leadership instincts, and as a football quarterback, a good grasp of how to guide a team. Ray was about the same size as Sailors and when Sailors came out for a rest, Ray played. Jim Collins was usually the first replacement at forward and Sailors believes he could have started for most teams. Shelton didn't substitute much, so if you weren't among the starting five, you didn't get a huge amount of playing time.

Wyoming's first game in the NCAA tournament took place on March 26 against the Oklahoma Sooners in Kansas City. It was a close game, but the Cowboys prevailed, 53–50. Defensively, the key was keeping Oklahoma scorer Gerald Tucker, the high point man in the Midlands Conference, under control. That was a tournament quarterfinal game. By winning, Wyoming advanced to a semifinal game against Texas. The Longhorns had defeated Washington, 59–55. Sailors called the matchup versus Texas Wyoming's toughest of the tournament.

The Cowboys had to overcome a 26–13 first-half deficit and the point-collecting prowess of the Longhorns' John Harris, who scored 29 points. Wyoming did not take its first lead until 37–36 on a Floyd Volker basket. In the closing minutes Volker fouled out and after falling behind by 5 points, Texas three times closed within a single point. Komenich led Wyoming with 17 points, Weir scored 13, and Sailors added 12.

Meanwhile, in the East Georgetown handled NYU, 55–36, while DePaul toppled Dartmouth, 46–35.

Chicago-based DePaul was led by a new, young coach, a former Notre Dame player, named Ray Meyer. Meyer took the reins for the Blue Demons in 1942 and remained head coach until 1984, compiling a 724–354 record. A Hall of Fame coach, Meyer, who died in 2006 at ninety-two, was always impressed by what he saw from Sailors during his playing days and the way he mastered the jump shot before others.

"There's a lot of people who say they shot it before him," Meyer said in the 1980s about Sailors being the pioneer of the shot. "There's one right here in Chicago who says he shot it in 1925. But if he did, he didn't jump over two inches. Kenny went up in the air. Kenny was the jump shooter that we know today. He got off the floor."

Unlike the modern college game, teams had no thirty-five-second shot clock to worry about. If Wyoming had a close game—and that was rare enough that year—it simply tried to hold possession and run out the clock. The Cowboys gave the ball to Sailors and let him dribble around until time expired.

"Lots of times they tried to trap me and I didn't even have to give the ball to anyone, I could just dribble past them," Sailors said. "Teams tried to trap me at half-court, but it didn't work. I don't remember getting trapped really.

I may have, but I don't remember. I don't remember anyone taking the ball away from me."

After polishing off the two foes in Kansas City, the Cowboys, Sailors, and the jump shot qualified for a trip to New York to play for the NCAA championship. The winner of the other bracket was Georgetown, which edged DePaul, 53-49.

"We were off by train to play the championship game at Madison Square Garden," Sailors said. "We were scheduled to play Georgetown and we didn't know anything about them. There were no TV games in those days. There was no scouting film either. Shelton talked to other coaches about them. That's the way it worked. He had a lot of coaching friends around the country. It was secondhand scouting, not like it is today. Everything is different than it was."

Wyoming boarded that east-bound train immediately after capturing the West playoff, the sweat barely dry on the Cowboys' bodies as they chugged toward New York. One thing that was going to be different for those eastern basketball fans was getting a glimpse of the jump shot as practiced by Kenny Sailors. Neither they, nor the Georgetown Hoyas, had seen anything like it before.

For the Cowboys, playing in New York, playing at Madison Square Garden, it was more returning to a friendly arena rather than entering an intimidating venue bringing with it a raft of unknowns. Wyoming had experience at the Garden and had sampled New York's entertainment before and was not wide-eyed enough to be sidetracked by any distractions.

Actually, the Cowboys usually stood out in Manhattan because they dressed like cowboys, per the request of promoter Ned Irish. That meant wearing cowboy hats, boots, and rodeo-style shirts.

"I'd have worn my spurs, if they let me," said Sailors, who even recalled one newspaper headline reading "WYOMING COWBOYS COME TO NEW YORK."

Once, the Cowboys even attended the Metropolitan Opera wearing flannel shirts and cowboy boots—no hats on that time—when the other men at the show were wearing tuxedos.

"People were rubbing their eyes, wondering who these punk kids were," Sailors said. "'They don't know anything about this kind of music.' They could tell we weren't New Yorkers. You know, I did enjoy it. I learned a lot."

Dressing like Old West characters contributed to the publicity for Wyoming's Garden games. Once in New York the Cowboys were walking four across on the crowded sidewalk, just being contrary as they paraded through Times Square. Some big fella approached Komenich, who was walking on the outside, put his arm around him and whispered in his ear. Next thing everyone knew the unwelcome visitor, who had propositioned Komenich, was lying flat on the cement. Apparently the outfits had provided the wrong impression about the players' sexual orientation.

"People didn't talk about it like they do today," Sailors said.

By the time Wyoming reached the national championship game Sailors said the players were somewhat cocky. Shelton tried to keep them humble, but their confidence was as high as the Empire State Building. They did remember the coach's words, though: "Lookee, boys, if you keep your head screwed on straight, you can beat anybody."

The Cowboys had already been the toast of New York once during the season, way back in December, had conquered their Skyline Conference opponents, and put away the NCAA foes in Kansas City. Either way, win or lose, Wyoming was going to open and close on Broadway in one night. This showdown against Georgetown was a one-night-only show, winner take all.

CHAPTER 6

National Champs

THE *LIFE* MAGAZINE PHOTOGRAPH OF KENNY SAILORS taking a jump shot against Georgetown on the cover of the March 30, 1943, issue makes it appear as if he has special superpowers compared to the rest of the men around him.

Sailors is elevated, seemingly two feet straight up off the ground, black sneakers dangling from a dangerous height while every other single person in the photograph, whether they are Wyoming teammates, Georgetown players, referees, or fans, are grounded. The fans are seated, the others are sprinkled around the Madison Square Garden court, but no one else is leaping, not the defender on Sailors, or the offensive or defensive players jockeying for position.

The message in the photo is that Sailors is flying while the rest of the world is flat-footed, even if he wasn't wearing a cape. And that essentially sums up how alien the jump shot was in the world of basketball at the time. While no one really knew it at the time Sailors was playing a different game than they were. He represented the game of the future while they represented the game of the past.

It was not an overnight change, but a gradual and steady one over the coming years, throughout the 1940s and early 1950s, leading into the 1960s. By then there were was almost no one left playing professional basketball who even experimented with a set shot.

The NCAA title game foe, Georgetown, like the other teams Wyoming encountered that winter, had never seen anyone so daringly throw up a long-range shot while leaving his feet. What Sailors did was heretical and the expert strategists did not think it was particularly wise because jumping off the floor meant that he had to be off-balance—and everyone knew that was all wrong.

It was a bit like finding out that the world was round, not flat, as everyone had previously assumed.

In later decades, under a brilliant, often-times grumpy, but highly principled coach named John Thompson, who had been a backup center for the Boston Celtics after graduating from Providence College, Georgetown attained a special stature in college basketball. It was regarded as one of the finest programs in the country and such future professional stars as Patrick Ewing, Alonzo Mourning, Greg Monroe, and Roy Hibbert are among its best-known hoop representatives.

Georgetown first competed in basketball in 1907, but the 1943 team reached new heights by qualifying for the NCAA championship game. Still, it was Wyoming that claimed the big prize and the main reason was the play of guard Kenny Sailors. In a low-scoring game, Sailors was the player who stood out most significantly.

Wyoming captured the title, 46–34, and Sailors scored 16 points. He was the only double-figure scorer in the game and his jump shot was the sensation of the day. Georgetown did all it could to slow him down, but mostly just slowed down the game. It was just 18–16 at halftime. The game was tied five times in the first half and five times in the second half, but Georgetown did sneak out to a 31–26 lead before the Cowboys put the Hoyas away in the closing minutes.

The reason for the final spread was attributed to Sailors by the United Press International observer on the scene who wrote, "Only Sailors' guidance and coolness in the fading moments turned it into a rout before the final gun."

Sailors respected Georgetown, but also never wavered in the belief that Wyoming was better.

"They were a good ball club," Sailors said, indicating that the final score was not indicative of the tightness of the game. "It seemed as if we beat them pretty handily, but they weren't a bad team. We played control ball and occasionally threw in a fast break."

The 1-3-1 Wyoming offense seemed to flummox Georgetown. Sailors had the ball out front and with Milo Komenich and Jim Weir spread on the wings and the Hoyas not adjusting, there was frequently open space to drive.

"Usually, there was nobody under there," Sailors said.

So the advice of Shelton echoing in his ears, Sailors consistently drove for the basket. Wyoming's second leading scorer that night was Collins with 8 points. When the game ended, the final buzzer sounding, the Cowboys reacted with surprising mildness. They didn't mob one another at half-court. They didn't

A team picture of the 1942–43 NCAA championship team without the players identified. Kenny is standing in the middle row wearing No. 4. (Photo courtesy the University of Wyoming.)

scream or jump up and down. They responded fairly calmly, almost as if this was just another ball game and the national championship hadn't been settled.

"We began to realize it as the clock ran down that we were going to win the national championship," Sailors said, "but when the game ended we didn't do much shouting or jumping. Shelton didn't tolerate any of that. He just patted me on the back and said, 'Nice game, Kenny. Nice game.' That was about it. We were all happy, but we didn't show much emotion, not on the court. We showed a little bit more when we got into our locker room."

Before they vacated the court, the presentation of the Most Outstanding Player was made, and the winner was Kenny Sailors. He was presented with the Chuck Taylor medal to commemorate the honor.

A torrent of praise poured down on Sailors after his showing in the NCAA title game, some from opponents, some from coaches, and some from sportswriters.

"He's the fastest man I ever tried to guard," said Georgetown back-court man Billy Hassett, who was assigned to shadow Sailors. "I was told to guard him close, but he was like an eel in there. He's the best I've been up against all year. I played him close when he came in, but then I had to give him room because you can't tell if he's going around you or going to shoot. He's great, that's all."

Another Georgetown player on that team was a freshman named Henry Hyde, who later became a prominent Congressman from Illinois. He was blown away by Sailors's shooting style. "Kenny Sailors was their star, their gun," Hyde said years later. "He had a deadly shot."

This game is when Ray Meyer, the DePaul coach, had his first sighting of Sailors in action.

"He's one of the best I've ever seen," Meyer said after Wyoming copped the title, "and I mean in playmaking above all. He's the boy who sets everything up."

The accolades piled up for Sailors and famed sportswriter W. C. Heinz collected several of the comments in his *New York Sun* article. Besides the Meyer observation, Manhattan Coach Joseph Daher said of Sailors, "He's as good a man as ever walked out on the Garden court. That kid's great."

St. John's Coach Joe Lapchick, who was to see plenty of Sailors in the coming days and coming years on various basketball courts said, "He's one of the best to ever show here."

Sailors naturally got some attention because of his jump shot, too. Louis Effrat, a *New York Times* sportswriter, commented on his skills. "His ability to dribble through and around any type of defense was uncanny," Effrat wrote, "just as was his electrifying one-handed shot."

All of the postmortems highlighted Sailors's leadership and play. A sportswriter for *New York PM* named Joe Cummiskey seemed to be smitten by love at first sight. "This Sailors can do anything with a basketball but tie a seaman's knot," Cummiskey wrote, "and given time and a chance to dribble two steps, he'd probably be able to do that. Sailors was the hand who held the S.S. *Wyoming* together. I wonder if Georgetown has ever heard of that old sea chantey entitled, 'Sailors Beware'?"

While the gaggle of sportswriters typed their reports on the situation as it occurred at Madison Square Garden, the Cowboys retreated to their Manhattan hotel. A bigger celebration awaited the Cowboy players back at their accommodations that night. Among the guests were several of Wyoming's most powerful politicians, United States senators, a Congressman, and "the big feed," as Sailors called it, was a big party. Almost as if it was a senior prom–type of event, a beautiful young lady was assigned to each player to keep him company through the evening's dinner. The job did not involve going back to their room to keep them company there.

"The girls sat next to us for conversation," Sailors said. "Later, my girlfriend, Bokie, saw a picture of that and she didn't like that too well."

The setting sounds a bit quaint, and in this modern era, an NCAA champion team might be whisked back to its hometown on the same night, though certainly no later than the next morning, to celebrate on campus with friends. The NCAA title game is also the apex of the season marking the end of the college basketball campaign begun many months earlier.

Only this particular year there was a twist. The National Invitation Tournament, always identified with Madison Square Garden, had begun in 1938, a year before the NCAA tournament. For many years they were competing national events of similar prestige and at this early point in the history of the two competitions, it was not clear whether winning an NCAA crown or winning an NIT crown was of more significance.

Because Wyoming was already in New York, and the NIT champion was St. John's of New York, it was determined that the winner of the two classic tournaments would play against each other a few days later to crown a true college champion. Naturally, the game would take place at the Garden. As a bow toward the worldwide conflagration, the proceeds from these ticket sales were donated to the Red Cross.

So although Wyoming was already named the NCAA champ, it faced St. John's to more or less unify the championship for 1943 the way future boxers would be torn between recognition by competing sanctioning bodies in their sport and fight to unify weight-class crowns.

St. John's has had a long and successful basketball tradition. Joe Lapchick, a member of the Original Celtics, was the team's coach at the time, during a tenure that extended from 1937 to 1947, before he became the floor boss of the New York Knicks. Later, Lapchick returned to St. John's for an extended second stint as coach, ending in 1965. A distinguished man who had been an exceptional player, his work put St. John's on the college basketball map.

During this time period St. John's teams were called the Redmen. The school subsequently changed its nickname to Red Storm.

Coach Lou Carnesecca later played a major role in raising the New York school's profile. St. John's experienced some great seasons affiliated with the Big East in more recent years. Sharp-shooting Chris Mullin is probably the best player in school history. No school, however, was more closely identified with the glory days of the NIT. St. John's owns a record six titles in the NIT.

The 1942–43 Redmen were a formidable collection, finishing with a 21-3 record. The St. John's duo of guard Hy Gotkin (8.3 points a game) and 6-foot-9 center Harry Boykoff (16.6 points a game) were called "Mutt and Jeff." Boykoff won the Most Valuable Player award in the NIT. St. John's crushed Toledo, 48–27, in the NIT championship game.

A third guard, Andrew "Fuzzy" Levane, who also averaged 8.3 points a contest, would actually have a brighter future in the sport. After playing pro ball, Levane coached the Knicks. In '43, though, he won the Haggerty Award as the MVP in the New York Metropolitan area.

St. John's had been invited to the NCAA tournament, but chose the hometown NIT instead. Now an intriguing bragging rights game had been concocted. As Sailors recalled it, the New York City newspapers did not give Wyoming as much credit as Shelton felt his Cowboys deserved, essentially proclaiming St. John's the true college champions of the season. There was probably some homerism involved, local boosterism, but Shelton was not happy that his NCAA crown was not equated with an NIT crown. It was always important to him to be well thought of in New York and this attack diminished his guys.

"They were crucifying us in the New York papers," Sailors said, "saying that the NCAA was a new league and the NIT had been going before they ever came into existence and on and on. They were telling why we weren't really the national champs. Shelton went to Ned Irish and said, 'We'll promote a game right here if they have the guts to play us. We'll play them right here in New York in Madison Square Garden.'"

"Irish jumped on it," Sailors said. But Shelton said he could not keep his team in New York more than a couple more days so the game would have to be scheduled swiftly. He also told Irish that the promoter would have to pay for the Cowboys' hotel and meal expenses if they stayed. Irish eagerly ponied up the cash.

Joe Lapchick didn't retreat from the challenge, either. He said, "Oh, we'll play them."

"They weren't afraid of us," Sailors said. "They really thought they could beat us. The press was telling them that they could. Every day the press was saying how much better the tournament was that they won than the one we won. And they were the home team. But we had played a lot in the Garden. We only played nine homes that year in Laramie. We were used to being on the road. Shelton was reading the newspapers and he said, 'Let's settle this once and for all.' He didn't like the idea of the papers putting down the NCAA and Wyoming."

Irish, who was the can-do organizer in the sport, pulled the entire event together quickly and two days later, on April 1, Wyoming and St. John's met in a charity game that attracted more than eighteen thousand fans. Indeed, the contest was much like a heavyweight boxing title unification match, though with a bit less hype over a shorter period of lead-up time.

Syndicated columnist Bob Considine was one writer who touted the matchup as a fitting end to the college season. He figured that the key to the result would be the inside play between Milo Komenich and Boykoff, describing them as "the two best big men in the game." He also cited Sailors and Levane as "two P-T boats protecting them" and predicted that those two guards would put on a "scampering duel that should be a good side attraction."

It was estimated by Considine, and later reported, that the game would provide $26,000 for the Red Cross. In contrast to the modern-day NCAA tournament where every game is televised live to every corner of the land, including Alaska and Hawaii (which, of course, weren't even close to becoming states yet in 1943), challenges had to be overcome in order to string enough wiring for the Cowboys games to be heard on radio in Wyoming.

The St. John's–Wyoming game was of more epic quality than the Wyoming-Georgetown game or the St. John's–Toledo game. Considine was correct in his advance analysis, since the forty-minute encounter did play out as a battle of big men. The Cowboys' Komenich pumped in 20 points and the Redmen's Boykoff scored 17 points.

One difference maker for Wyoming was forward Jim Weir, who scored 13 points. But Sailors was the key guard in the game, adding 11 points and drawing defenders away from Komenich so he could make his low-post specialty shots. Yet the teams were evenly matched and were tied after regulation play. It took an overtime session for Wyoming to outlast St. John's, 52–47.

"We played them and we never heard another word about them being better than us," Sailors said. "That was the end of it. They were good. They were better than Georgetown, I think. They had guards that were good, but they didn't have a jump shot the way I did. That gave me a big advantage. They were still shooting the set shot. It was a good game. They tied it at the end in regulation."

There was some controversy near the end of the game when Matt Kennedy, who was a famous referee at the time, whistled a foul on Wyoming and was booed by the Garden crowd.

"When he called 'Foul!' he'd point his finger at you," Sailors said. "He'd blow that whistle and his cheeks would puff out. You didn't have any doubts that you were the one who had committed the foul."

When the game ended, once again the Cowboys were feted at a splendid dinner, this time at the Waldorf Astoria.

And again, as the players dined in high style, the sportswriting witnesses were banging out comments singing about the magnificence of the University of Wyoming basketball club in general and Kenny Sailors in particular.

Some of the compliments might even have made Sailors blush, such as the words chosen by the *Sporting News* correspondent, who as a writer for a

Kenny goes after a loose ball while being guarded by St. John's Hy Gotkin. Wyoming's center, no. 17 Milo Komenich, can be seen just behind them. (Photo courtesy the University of Wyoming.)

weekly publication meshed his reportage of both the NCAA title game and the St. John's game into one story, saying, "Sailors was the darling of the Garden gallery. He put on a two-night display that was a combination of Sonja Henie in an ice ballet, Sid Luckman quarterbacking and forward passing, and Leopold Stokowski directing a symphony orchestra." Sailors should have had that printed on business cards and spent the rest of his life handing them out.

The writer, Cy Kritzer, continued: "Sailors has thin legs, wide shoulders and biceps and the long arms of a heavyweight wrestler. If it can be said a man has beautiful hands, Sailors has them. Once at quarter-court he used those hands like a virtuoso, and the Wyoming team responded to every move. Sailors was like a coach in action. It was a great duel between two superbly trained teams and Sailors was the difference."

Sailors was far from the biggest man on the court, but he was the fastest, with the best floor vision. He made the Cowboys go and Shelton made them into a cohesive unit that was clearly the best college team in the country. Once St. John's pretensions were put to bed, there were no more contenders.

"None in the crowd could dispute their right to the crown," Louis Effrat wrote in the *New York Times*. "This crew of rip-roaring, swashbuckling big men merited every honor, every handshake, and every backslap that came their way. And there were plenty on all sides."

After Wyoming stormed through New York, conquering Georgetown and St. John's, *Newsweek* magazine called Sailors a "Lilliputian . . . between his Brobdingnagian lieutenants" Komenich and Weir.

Writer Joe Cummiskey, who had become enamored of the Cowboys while covering the NCAA championship game, raved about the players again. "They called on Kenny Sailors, the dribbling fool," he wrote. "Big Boy Harry Boykoff met more than his match. Big Milo Komenich made him look like he was still in high school. Let's close with a long cheer for Wyoming. They earned it the hard way. I know now why someone once said, 'Go West, young man, go West.' He must have meant you might end up being a great basketball player."

Long Island University Coach Clair Bee, who was not only an esteemed coach, but the author of a series of sports books for boys featuring do-gooder character Chip Hilton, wrote about the Wyoming–St. John's game. He focused on the guard matchup between Sailors and St. John's Hy Gotkin.

"An important item in the Wyoming victory was the great playing of Ken Sailors," Bee wrote. "Coach Lapchick did a lot this season [with] his 'pony,' fast little Hy Gotkin, who went in to outspeed rivals, and did it against most clubs. But in Sailors Hy more than met his match. The 'Whippet' was outrun last night."

Not only was Sailors named the Most Valuable Player for Wyoming in the NCAA tournament, but he was honored on a smorgasbord of All-American teams starting as an undergraduate and especially culminating this year. The *Sporting News, True* magazine, Chuck Taylor, the AAU, and the Helms Foundation heaped recognition on Sailors. He also was the Sullivan Award winner for his region, the honor that anoints the best amateur athlete in the country each year. That made him a national finalist, although Sailors did not win.

It has been said that if you can make it in New York you can make it anywhere, and although that phrase was coined later Wyoming had indeed made it big in New York. There was a glow of satisfaction and pride surrounding the team as it boarded the train home to Laramie.

CHAPTER 7

The Jump
Shot's Evolution

WHEN KENNY SAILORS SHOWED OFF HIS JUMP SHOT at Madison Square Garden in New York City in the NCAA title game in March of 1943, and against St. John's in early April, almost no one in the stands or on the sidelines had seen anybody take such a weird shot at the basket.

Many people didn't know what to make of it. Not everyone approved. Few realized that it represented the shot of the future as basketball, then a half century old, matured as a game. What they did know was that the shot seemed revolutionary and that this Sailors guy made many of his baskets in this manner, which defied logic to them.

To some extent taking a jump shot instead of a set shot was like swimming with your head in the water instead of above the surface, or throwing a forward pass instead of handing the ball off to a fellow member of the backfield in football.

Joe Lapchick, who at the time was St. John's coach, watched the jump shot become a deadly weapon for players during his tenure with the Redmen, then with the New York Knicks of the NBA, and finally back at St. John's. In 1965, Lapchick said, "Sailors started the one-hand jumper, which is probably the shot of the present and the future."

Over the last eighty years, various sources have labeled Sailors as being "the inventor" of the jump shot. He never used the description because he realized some stranger somewhere must have left his feet to take a shot at a hoop in another backyard or on another playground.

"I don't say that I'm the first guy who ever shot a jump shot," Sailors has said many times in similar ways. "I'm sure there must be some kid somewhere who jumped in the air and shot the ball somewhere. But the old-timers credit me with it."

There is no question of Sailors's pedigree with the jump shot dating to the 1930s in those one-on-one games against brother Bud. No one else was using a jump shot as part of his repertoire in high school contests or college games until Sailors came along either. Not the jump shot that we know today. Not the jump shot as it is portrayed on the NBA logo, which borrowed the silhouetted form from future star Jerry West.

There have been other claimants to the early use of the jump shot, but there has never been solid proof that anyone else used the jump shot in the manner Sailors did before he did. There has never been solid proof that anyone else used the jump shot as it is known, used, and taught today in the sport before Sailors, either.

A wide variety of sources, from eyewitnesses such as Lapchick and DePaul Coach Ray Meyer, to books and websites, ascribe the jump shot's beginnings to Sailors. It is not something that can be copyrighted or patented in a United States government office, but is more like folklore, passed on through generations by word of mouth from a time when basketball games were not filmed like documentaries and photographers attended few contests.

A 1994 *New York Times* story headlined "The Birth of the Jump Shot" was actually a review of a book called *Big Leagues: Professional Baseball, Football, and Basketball in National Memory.* The book's author, Stephen Fox, contended that "sports history unreels around a circle, not down a line." He also stated that the addition of the lively ball to baseball, the forward pass in football, and the jump shot in basketball all contributed mightily to the popularity of those sports.

When it comes to defining the jump shot it is simplistically explained as usually being a shot with a basketball taken when a player jumps in the air— normally straight up. Of course, variations of jump shots being taken off-balance abound now.

Sailors offered his definition of how to make optimum use of the shot in an article that was written for NCAA.com in 2013.

"You don't shoot it on the way up, you don't shoot it on the way down," he said. "You have to take the shot right at the peak of your jump. It takes a little practice. It's all wrists and fingers when you release it."

Although later in life Sailors couldn't remember a date when he attempted his first jump shot against his brother he has given enough interviews over the years that others have tried to pinpoint it for him and concluded that it was probably in May of 1934. He was in junior high school at the time, Bud in high school. No spectators were present—unless mom looked out the window of the house. It was hardly a eureka moment for her when she would have rushed outside and tried to capture the moment with a camera.

Basketball was invented in 1891 by Dr. James Naismith and it was a static, floor-bound game. The first players shot at a peach basket and when someone made a shot by heaving the ball skyward, the game paused for an official to dig the ball out of the wooden basket.

Eventually, the hoop was invented, a net was placed on it, and when players made a shot it fell through to the floor. Throughout the 1920s and beyond, it was felt that the most efficient way to make an outside shot was to stand still and throw the ball at the basket with two hands on it to accurately guide it. Good players could make shots from thirty feet away, but they never left their feet when propelling the ball to the ten-foot-high rim.

For many years, casual basketball observers gave credit to Stanford All-American Hank Luisetti for inventing the jump shot. Luisetti, who was born in 1916 in San Francisco, rather invented a shot that was an intermediary shot between the set shot and jump shot. Luisetti featured a running one-hander. He charged toward the foul line on his dribble, cocked the ball behind his ear, and let fly, though his feet did not leave the ground.

Luisetti, who stood 6-foot-2 and weighed 185 pounds, was twice named college basketball's player of the year and was chosen All-American three times. On January 1, 1938, in a game played in Cleveland against Duquesne, Luisetti became the first college player to score 50 points in a game. That night he made twenty-three field goals and four free throws as Stanford won, 92–27.

Like Sailors, Luisetti had to travel to New York for a game to receive maximum exposure and publicity for his shot. "He revolutionized shooting," Mike Montgomery, who decades later was Stanford's coach, told the *Stanford Magazine*. "Someone would have come up with [a one-handed shot], somewhere along the line, but he was the guy who was first and he had tremendous success with it. Once he started shooting like that people said, 'Oh, you *can* do that,' and it became the way everybody did it."

Not quite. Few shot exactly like Luisetti with his running start. There were definitely detractors, too, who felt Luisetti was out of control and did not want to see their players using any such recklessness in a game. Interestingly, one of those critics was Nat Holman, then the coach of City College of New York, who had been a Lapchick teammate with the Original Celtics.

"That's not basketball," Holman said. "If my boys ever shot one-handed, I'd quit coaching."

Before he had seen Sailors's jumper, Lapchick also was skeptical about Luisetti's method of making shots.

"I can't be persuaded that two [hands] on the ball doesn't make for far superior shot control and a greater percentage of hits," Lapchick said in the early 1940s.

While Luisetti did not adapt his game because of a bigger brother who was swatting all of his shots away, he did have his reason for trying a one-handed shot in place of the two-hand set.

"Shooting two-handed, I just couldn't reach the basket," he said.

What Montgomery said of Luisetti, others said of Sailors. What Luisetti said of himself, Sailors said of himself. They were both innovators during a period of time when basketball was mostly played below the rim.

"I was lucky with my coaches in high school and college, I guess," Luisetti said. "Because I made the baskets they left me alone and didn't try to change my shots."

Luisetti had a phenomenal college basketball career, but he came along before there was an NBA and professional leagues were not yet stable, or did not offer reasonable salaries. Luisetti, who died at eighty-six in 2002, continued playing basketball with the Phillips 66 AAU team.

Sailors did see Luisetti play in an AAU tournament in Denver and Luisetti's style influenced him. By then Sailors already had the rudiments of his jumper down—the games against Bud were years in the past. But Sailors also tinkered with his shot off and on over the years trying to improve his accuracy.

Several decades later Sailors wished to both credit Luisetti and differentiate his own shot from the Stanford player's. "Luisetti had a step-and-shoot move," Sailors said. "I think that's where I copied the one-hand shot from him." But, as he noted, Luisetti didn't jump in the air, clearing the floor with both feet as he shot.

One reason that Sailors jumped was because he could jump. That is, he was a strong leaper with a thirty-six-inch vertical leap. That meant that when he jumped he was outjumping most people.

A later Wyoming coach, Jim Brandenburg, who became friends with Sailors, came out of Texas and said he first became aware of the jump shot when the Cowboys made headlines with their romp to the NCAA crown. The jump shot enthralled people, he said in a book called *Cowboy Up* about Wyoming basketball, but "it wasn't like Kenny went to New York and everybody started shooting the jump shot. It took a while for coaches to get used to it. Coaches did not have a progressive set of skills they would teach. Once the cat was out of the bag and the jump shot was introduced, it has become such a predominant part of the game. Kenny was a tremendous athlete, and I truly think he is the guy who should be fully credited for the innovation of the jump shot."

Author John Christgau penned a book called *The Origins of the Jump Shot* featuring eight players who were early jump shooters. In Christgau's opinion all eight played a role in introducing the jump shot to basketball.

Christgau grew up in Minnesota and remembered seeing a Brainerd High School player named Myer "Whitey" Skoog shoot a jump shot in 1944. Skoog was later a guard for the great Minneapolis Lakers champions of the NBA. For much the same reason that Sailors perfected his jump shot versus his taller brother, Skoog attempted one jumper over a taller opposing center on Bemidji in the third quarter of a game. It was the last jump shot he took for five years, however, when he was then playing for the University of Minnesota. In part because he felt as if was a "hot dog" or "show-off" for taking the off-balance heave.

In research for his book, Christgau suggested that John "Mouse" Gonzalez of San Francisco said he took a jump shot at a YMCA for the first time in October of 1942 and that Dave Minor took jump shots for Gary, Indiana, between 1937 and 1941 in high school games.

Interestingly, in the book, Curt Gowdy, the same man who was a teammate of Sailors's at Wyoming, was quoted as saying that Johnny Adams of Arkansas was the first jump shooter he had seen when he played against him in 1941. That contradicts Gowdy's personal history with Sailors at Wyoming that predates the NCAA contest he referred to. Adams and Sailors were pretty much concurrent. In later years Sailors became aware of Adams's use of a similar shot.

"Luisetti didn't shoot a jump shot the way we know it," Sailors said. "He had one foot on the deck. Ray Meyer said, 'It wasn't a jump shot, Kenny.' Gowdy said that Johnny Adams shot the first jump shot in the game of basketball. I don't think anyone will ever know who really shot the first one. The game started in the 1800s. Some kid jumped in the air and shot the ball somewhere.

Ray Meyer and Joe Lapchick made it real clear that in New York when I shot it, that was the first."

Christgau's reporting indicated that Belus Van Smawley from North Carolina was using his jump shot perhaps as early as 1934, like Sailors. Smawley practiced taking jump shots at an abandoned train depot that had been turned into a court and that he and his friends used to play on in bad weather. Smawley's claim to fame was the turn-around jump shot first publicized during the 1942–43 season at Appalachian State. Smawley played just one season there and had his college attendance interrupted by World War II.

After the war, in 1946, he turned professional and competed for five seasons—actually almost perfectly overlapping with Sailors in pro ball.

"When I got in the pros the only guy in the league who shot anything like the jump shot that I did was Belus Smawley," Sailors said. "He had both feet off the floor, but he shot two-handed with the ball behind his head and fell back. He didn't use the height to shoot, he faded back. But he was off the floor. He was probably off the floor about eighteen inches. Height wasn't his objective.

"I covered him. He was good. He was tough. When he was hitting, boy, he was very tough to cover. When he wasn't hitting, he wasn't very tough to cover."

Bud Palmer, who died in March of 2013 at ninety-one, became a famous sportscaster and writer who also worked for Mayor John Lindsay of New York. Palmer was born in Hollywood, but attended Phillips Exeter Academy in New Hampshire and then Princeton. By 1939, the 6-foot-4 Palmer had employed the jump shot in high school games.

Palmer was later captain of the New York Knicks, but when he tried out for the team in 1946, his coach, Neil Cohalen, took one look at the aspiring Palmer's jump shot and said, "What the hell kind of shot is that?"

More famed than any of the others as a professional star was Joe Fulks. Nicknamed "Jumpin' Joe," Fulks came out of the small community of Birmingham, Kentucky, and used some kind of jump shot in high school in the 1930s.

Fulks was one of the first stars of the new NBA and led the league in scoring during the 1946–47 season, averaging 23.2 points per game. The next season he led the league again, averaging 22.1 points a game. He once scored a record 63 points in a game, a mark that stood from the 1948–49 season until the 1960–61 season when the Lakers' Elgin Baylor scored 71 points in a game.

For many years after Sailors left the college basketball spotlight and the pros, as well, he lived in a remote hand-built log cabin in Gakona, Alaska. He was out of sight and out of mind. He had little to do with the sport of his upbringing except coaching some high school ball. Some historians even acted as if he had died. At the least he had become invisible. Yet anytime a sportswriter somewhere wrote an article indicating that someone else had originated the jump shot, fans in Wyoming or elsewhere spoke up. Hey, wait a minute, they would say: Don't forget Kenny Sailors.

One writer who did not make the mistake of overlooking Sailors was Alexander Wolff, the *Sports Illustrated* basketball writer who authored a book entitled *100 Years of Hoops* that came out in 1991 to celebrate the anniversary of the invention of the game.

In a section of the book labeled "The Shot," an item read, "1940: Kenny Sailors of Wyoming is credited with being the first player to use the jump shot in college competition. Sailors will be tournament MVP as the Cowboys win the 1943 NCAA title." In the accompanying text, Wolff wrote, "Wyoming's Kenny Sailors is widely credited with birthing the jumper (later to be called the J)."

Sailors has always been modest about his role. He eschews the description of inventor of the jump shot, but accepts the blessing of others who say that he first took the shot that most approximates the modern jumper and that his use of it helped popularize it. Sailors said Fulks was more athletic than he was and "is the individual who fine-tuned the shot."

When it comes to talking about the invention of the jump shot, it is not as neat to compare it to, say, the invention of the lightbulb, where Thomas Edison's is the only name mentioned.

However, when Kenny Sailors was inducted into the College Basketball Hall of Fame in November of 2012, one of the main reasons cited during the ceremony was his "invention of the jump shot."

It was the final stamp of approval of the role he played in the evolution of the sport that he loved.

Sailors began shooting the jump shot in 1934. He used the jump shot in high school and he brought the jump shot to college at Wyoming in the autumn of 1939. He didn't play varsity ball until the fall of 1940, and that's when the first photos of him taking a jump shot were clicked.

"I've got pictures of me shooting it my sophomore year," he said. "Then I shot it more my junior year."

Longtime Wyoming sportswriter and broadcaster, the late Larry Birleffi, attended the school at the same time Sailors did and always remembered the hours of practice the guard put in with extra time gym visits. Birleffi said Sailors seemed to always be in the gym working out, jumping up and down and shooting hundreds of those newfangled shots.

"We thought it was a little radical really," Birleffi said years later. But he said that work paid off for the hustling guard from Hillsdale and that by the time Sailors finished his schooling at Wyoming "he was a household name."

In his nineties, Sailors has a good memory, but after the passage of so many years, while he can envision that very first jump shot taken against Bud he cannot recall with 100 percent certainly whether or not it went in the basket. And Lord, he has tried many times to recall that. He won't fudge it, though, if he can't remember and tell someone that yes, indeedy, the shot hit the spot, although he did so when he was much younger.

"As near as I can remember," Sailors said, "I just dribbled up to him and I just jumped as high as I could in the air."

For all intents and purposes, the stop-action camera should have stopped there. These days someone would have been standing close by with a camera phone and posted the photo of the grand moment on the Internet. It would have been a YouTube sensation, going viral, within hours.

Instead, only words preserve the happenings on the hard court of 1934.

CHAPTER 8

Back in Wyoming

WHILE KENNY SAILORS SAID THE REASON HE AND HIS TEAMMATES did not celebrate excessively on the Madison Square Garden court after they won both of their big games was the background of World War II and the fact that they all might soon be going to war, no such inhibitions were evident in Laramie.

When the Cowboys debarked from the train from New York it seemed the entire city was on hand to greet them and fete them. Laramie threw one of the grandest parties it ever had. The reception began when the players spilled from the train and it continued for two days, though in some ways it never completely ceased.

"They put us all up on fire trucks and had a parade," Sailors said. "They did that two different times, the same thing each day, driving us all over town on the fire trucks. The schools were closed. The stores were closed. Everything was closed up."

There was nothing so satisfying as being treated as kings by the home folks.

"They had us sitting up there on the fire wagons, sirens going, people standing outside along the streets everywhere in town," Sailors said. "People drove up and down the streets, too, and yelled at us, called out our names. I swear, pretty much for a year after we won that championship I couldn't pay a bill in a restaurant. I'd go in to buy a sweater or anything in a clothing store and they'd give it to me."

These days they call those perks NCAA rules violations, but the NCAA rule book was probably fifty pages thick back then, not a thousand.

The trophy that the Cowboys earned for winning the college championship still reposes in the campus trophy case and it stands two feet tall. It's not a shrinking violet award and it probably gets more attention than any other school sports honor in that case. Actually the trophy was so big that Wyoming Coach Everett Shelton couldn't figure out the best way to carry it home on the train.

He told officials, "Well, how do you expect me to lift that?" So NCAA officials shipped it to the University of Wyoming. The other trophy that came home to Laramie was Sailors's MVP honor and nobody in that city ever forgot that individual triumph either.

Still, many years later forward Floyd Volker was dismayed to read in the Casper newspaper how maybe the 1943 Cowboys weren't all that great and how modern athletes would have thumped them. He whipped out pen and paper and wrote a letter to the editor that in part read, "I agree that today's players are bigger, stronger, and perhaps faster than yesterday's—but better? Despite the fact that most of us worked for our room and board, didn't have special diets, camps, videos, and sometimes played games after driving all night to get there, we managed to accomplish more than any Wyoming team has since, against as formidable to us as teams Wyoming faces today are to them. So please, compare us if you will, but don't put us down. I still think Kenny Sailors could do anything any player can do today—and maybe better."

It was April when the season ended, and the end of the school year was approaching. Coming at the players much faster, however, was the war. Sailors had been a member of the ROTC (Reserve Officers' Training Corps) program at Wyoming, so he knew he was going into the service.

"I already had my commission because I was one of the top leaders in the Wyoming ROTC program," Sailors said. "But the Marines—they did it all the time—gave a permanent second lieutenant commission to one successful person in the ROTC unit. They let me call the battalion to attend and gave me that regular commission. Nearly all of us were lined up to go somewhere."

Jim Collins and Floyd Volker were also joining the Marines. The Marines let the Wyoming players finish out the basketball season before reporting. Sailors was sure it was done for good publicity, for military recruiting reasons.

"The Marines are smart in doing that," he said. "I had a big name in sports at the time and they thought I could do them a lot of good recruiting. They didn't want me to get killed. They could have sent me to Iwo Jima. But we knew we were going somewhere as soon as the basketball season ended."

Kenny Sailors, USMC, with Marilynne, February 22, 1944. The photo was taken by Kenny's father-in-law B. H. Corbin, a freelance photographer. (Photo courtesy Kenny Sailors.)

Sailors's first stop was going to be at the Marine Corps base at Quantico, Virginia. By then Sailors and Marilynne were planning their marriage. They had only dated for less than a year, but were confident they would be good life mates, and they had become formally engaged. Sailors completed the training program at Quantico. He was then scheduled to be stationed in San Diego as his next stop, but in-between he got married. Sailors was married wearing his Marine uniform. The wedding took place in July. It was not a major-league ceremony with hundreds of people. The war saw to that.

The site of the marriage was in the tiny town of Frannie, Wyoming, in the northwest corner of the state. Marilynne's parents were working there for the railroad. Her father was a dispatcher and her mother delivered messages to trains passing through.

The United States declared war on Japan immediately after the Pearl Harbor attack of December 7, 1941, and by mid-1943 the country's focus was on little else but the conflict in Asia and Europe and wherever it spread. Young men were being killed in battles conducted in places on the globe that until weeks or even days before had never been heard of by American citizens. By the time Sailors left for assignment in San Diego he had friends who had perished in the war.

"It is hard to explain to anyone who wasn't living at the time, but our minds were no longer on basketball," Sailors said. "We knew we were going in the service. I'd already lost buddies. A fraternity brother had been taken on Bataan. More than seventy thousand American and Filipino soldiers had been captured by the Japanese. A friend of mine made that death march and he lost both of his legs.

"I think us winning the basketball championship did make people feel good for a little while in Wyoming. Maybe it took their minds off the war for a bit. I think Collins and Volker might have gone into the Marines because of me and because I already knew I was going. Jim Weir was headed to Europe. Lew Roney also went to the Atlantic. Milo Komenich was too tall and so he didn't go into the service."

Perhaps the oddest aspect of that spring was that as a gesture of respect for those going off to fight, some of the players, including Sailors, were graduated ahead of schedule. He had been enrolled at Wyoming since 1939, participated as a player as a freshman, even though it was not varsity competition, and then played his sophomore year of 1940–41, junior year of 1941–42, and his senior year of 1942–43. He did not finish classes, but was given his degree in education. At the time Sailors geared his schooling toward a career as a teacher and high school coach.

"Spring quarter I was short eight or nine hours for my degree," Sailors said. "They went ahead and graduated me and Jim Weir, though they shouldn't have. They said we graduated when we really hadn't. That became a big issue later on."

For whatever reason—and Sailors believes it was because he had made a big name for himself in sports—the Marines were gentle with him. He never saw true combat. He was shipped to the South Pacific, though.

"They put me aboard a ship and it was dangerous because there were plenty of places where our ship could have been sunk," Sailors said. "The Zeroes

[Japanese fighter planes] could have hit us. But we had convoys and we came through it. Fortunately, I didn't get shot up. I think they kind of took care of me, the Marines did. In a way it wasn't right, probably, but they did it."

Sailors spent most of his service time aboard large ships that visited several South Pacific islands, such as Guam and Saipan. Their job was to pick up the wounded and take them out of harm's way. He rode a huge hospital ship. Sailors, who was promoted to captain during the war, commanded a detachment of between forty and fifty Marines.

"I went around the world twice," he said. "We were all over the world. Our first trip out we didn't return to the United States for about two years. We brought out thirty-five hundred to four thousand Army troops from San Pedro, California, and had nurses aboard that we were bringing to Calcutta, India."

The troops were replacements for men in New Guinea. That trip Sailors's ship traveled without escort.

"We were a new ship and we had as much speed as the battle wagons did," Sailors said. "The only way the Japanese could have ever shot at us, even with a submarine, from the water, was if they knew our route and were ahead waiting for us. There was no possible way they could catch us if we got ahead of them."

Once the ship was at sea, Sailors commanded the Marine unit that handled security. While most of the ship was a hospital, it was also big enough to carry those several thousand troops, too. Except for stopping at islands to transfer wounded personnel aboard, Sailors almost never set foot on land for nearly two years. While he was gone, Marilynne gave birth to the couple's first child, a girl named Linda.

The shipboard assignment did have its satisfactions for Sailors's Marines. They knew they were doing important work.

"We probably saved a lot of lives by picking up these kids that had a leg or an arm shot off," he said. "It wasn't a very pleasant job to see all of that suffering, but it was what our job was. We'd go ashore and spend the night in tents. We almost never came into contact with the Japanese, only when some stragglers who had escaped and not been killed were raiding the villages and stealing eggs, chickens, or hogs for food."

Sailors was not really shot at by the enemy and he was never in anything like hand-to-hand combat. At times he did have to lead his troop of men off the beaches to hunt down those few straggler Japanese battle survivors.

"I had to go with my men and take care of these single Japanese soldiers, or two or three of them, and round them up sometimes," he said. "They might retreat to a little cave and we had to smoke them out."

Like some other top athletes who were at American military installations, Sailors played his favorite sport at his base. Some military squads were famous for their talent and representing their branch of the service or their home bases. The play was not that serious in San Diego and although Sailors played some basketball at first, the commanding office, a three-star general, who had lost a son in the war, considered the idea of the men playing ball to be distasteful.

"He came out in the San Diego newspapers," Sailors said, "and said, 'What are we doing? Are we fighting a war, or are we playing basketball?' I was probably on that hospital ship within three weeks after he said that."

Compared to many, many others, Sailors had a relatively safe war and he knew it. When World War II ended and he was discharged, he returned to Laramie. Marilynne was still in school. The Cowboys had lost virtually the whole team to war service, so the school did not even field a squad for the 1943–44 season. Shelton did coach a team for the 1944–45 season, but it finished a mediocre 10–18.

When the players returned to campus—and all of them were safe, although Weir had been wounded—the Skyline Conference granted them all another year of eligibility because of the school time lost to military service. One by one the key players from the championship team returned and slipped on uniforms. Sailors was not back for the start of school, but by early 1946 he was playing ball for the Cowboys again.

The rather impressionable, yet unflappable country boys who had once been wide-eyed at seeing the bright lights of New York City were now much more mature young men and they had seen things in war that were much more strongly seared into their minds than what New York displayed.

Despite the time off, however, they were better players than ever. They were older and stronger and unlikely to be unduly bothered by anything that transpired in a mere game. As the players came back and meshed again as a unit Wyoming emerged as the No. 1 ranked college basketball team in the land. Those who voted in such polls realized who was on the roster and recognized that the same players that had been mere lads when they claimed a title might be even better.

Because Wyoming considered Sailors finished as an undergraduate student, he enrolled in graduate level courses. He missed some of the earliest games on the schedule, but before long was dribbling his way past defenders and shooting that darned jump shot again.

"We had practically the whole team back," Sailors said. "Weir wasn't what he had been because his shoulder had been shot up. He had shrapnel still in it. They never got it all out."

Wyoming got better and better as the year progressed and completed the regular season with a 22–4 record. The Cowboys were prepared to chase another NCAA title. That is, the Cowboys were convinced they could win another NCAA title—until the NCAA informed the school that several of its players were ineligible because they were graduate students.

"The big shots that run the show stepped in," Sailors said. "We shouldn't even have been graduate students, but the school had given us our credits and graduated us. The conference said we could play, so we didn't think a thing about it. Almost the whole team was in the same situation. So we were the No. 1 ranked team in the country, but we didn't even play in the NCAA tournament."

Sailors received All-American notoriety in 1943 and that season was chosen the college player of the year, in addition to earning AAU All-American recognition. In 1946 he was again voted a college All-American and was selected as the Helms Foundation player of the year. Sailors gained his honors that year more for his floor leadership and passing than his scoring since he averaged just 7.8 points a game.

He completed college play as a four-year letterman and a three-time Skyline Conference all-league performer.

And by then Sailors's fame began to spread as the originator of the shot that old-fashioned coaches couldn't stomach. With the jump shot he was ahead of his time, but now his forum had evaporated.

Although Sailors was twenty-five already by the time he completed his stay at Wyoming, his timing was pretty good because starting in 1946 there were new and better options available than ever before for a guy who wished to continue playing basketball and get paid for doing so.

On June 6, 1946, in New York City, the professional league was founded as the Basketball Association of America that within a few years would change its name to the National Basketball Association. Kenny Sailors was very interested in finding out just what this new league was all about.

CHAPTER 9

Going Pro

THE NATIONAL BASKETBALL ASSOCIATION IS THE YOUNGEST of the four major team sports leagues in the United States. Major League Baseball began in 1876 with the founding of the National League. The National Hockey League opened its doors for the 1917–18 season. The National Football League dates to an organizational meeting in 1920.

Pro basketball as we know it, as an organized, unified, continuing league, did not get its start until the fall of 1946. At the time the hoops league was known as the Basketball Association of America (BAA). There were two divisions, an East and a West, and the cities with teams included Washington, Philadelphia, New York, Providence, Toronto, Boston, Chicago, St. Louis, Cleveland, Detroit, and Pittsburgh. The champion of the fledgling league was the Philadelphia Warriors, led by sharpshooting Joe Fulks.

Far from a stable enterprise, the early days of this pro basketball league were marked by volatility. Franchises folded. Franchises switched cities. A competing National Basketball League (NBL), which had been founded in 1937 and had teams located in smaller cities, scrapped for its existence.

Unlike the BAA, the NBL had a different type of owner. While rich individuals led the way in the BAA, the NBL was created by businesses— General Electric, Firestone, and Goodyear. The teams were clustered in smaller cities dotted around the Midwest. When the BAA absorbed the NBL for the 1949–50 season the league played with seventeen teams and the composition only slightly resembled the original BAA locations.

That year teams competed in Syracuse (New York), New York City, Washington,

Philadelphia, Baltimore, Boston, Minneapolis, Rochester, Fort Wayne, Chicago, St. Louis, Indianapolis, Anderson (Indiana), Tri-Cities (Davenport, Iowa; Moline, Illinois; and Rock Island, Illinois), Sheboygan (Wisconsin), Waterloo (Iowa), and Denver.

This was very much a growing pains era for the league. Many of those cities would soon be left by the wayside as the NBA solidified and shrank to eight cities for most of the 1950s, producing a smaller league, but more stability.

Compared to the modern era, the game was more stagnant, with lower-scoring games, and grounded, with only a few individuals even trying to pass as jump shooters, including Kenny Sailors, throughout the player ranks. Eventually, the 24-second clock was added in 1954 to speed up play and prevent stalls, and over time every player in the league learned or acquired a jump shot until the set shot had virtually disappeared from competition by 1960. Only a few holdover players who had been weaned on it ever employed the tamer set shot as the game went vertical.

"There was a lot of attention on pro basketball at the time I finished school because the league was just getting started," Sailors said.

There was no player draft as was instituted later, so in essence Sailors, an All-American, was a free agent, able to sign with any team that made him the best offer. However, at the time the best offer a pro basketball team could muster unless it was for someone like George Mikan, the remarkable 6-foot-10 center out of DePaul who was considered the greatest big man of his era, was approximately $7,500.

"I could have had a career in the Marines," Sailors said. "But I wanted to go home and I wanted to play more basketball. I went to Cleveland because the Rebels gave me the most money."

That $7,500 salary seems puny now, but Sailors was wooed since it topped other offers. The Rochester Royals sent a representative to Wyoming to visit Sailors and then they paid his expenses to come to upstate New York to work out. The St. Louis Bombers also traveled to Wyoming to scout Sailors.

During Sailors's trip to Rochester, he ran into a famous athlete whom he had gotten to know during World War II. Otto Graham, an athlete from Northwestern, had played college ball, but was much better known for his prowess as a quarterback and Graham became a Hall of Fame quarterback for the Cleveland Browns based on his stardom for a decade starting in the late 1940s.

Graham had actually signed on with the Royals and played one season, but he was not pleased with the atmosphere surrounding the club. He feared its finances were shaky. Graham, who would soon take his own advice and not stick around, told Sailors, "Kenny, you don't want to play for this team." Sailors asked why not. He wanted to know if the Royals were going to be a bad team. "They've got a pretty fair team, but they haven't paid me my playoff money yet from last year," Graham said. "I don't know if they're broke, or what the deal is, but I haven't got it."

Graham was poised to abandon Rochester for the start of his football career in Cleveland and he thought that the owners of the Browns and the basketball team in Cleveland were connected and were on solid footing.

"I can take you over to whoever is the head of the basketball program and introduce you," Graham said. "I think Cleveland would be a pretty nice place to play in."

Sailors and Graham took the train together from Rochester to Cleveland. Graham became a legend for the football team and Sailors signed with the Cleveland Rebels basketball team.

"That's why I chose Cleveland," Sailors said. "He said, 'Come with me. I like it up there.' Sure enough Otto made the arrangements to get me the interview with the basketball people. Nice guy. I signed. They offered me more money than I'd been offered in Rochester or St. Louis or any of the other places that talked to me. It was a couple of thousand dollars more and in that day that was a lot of money."

The deal made Sailors the highest paid point guard in the league for the time being. The highest paid player of all was Mikan, who was making about $11,000. Whatever Mikan was being paid—and his salary went up from there— it was worth it to the league. He was such a big star that sometimes his name appeared on the marquee outside an arena above the name of the teams that were playing, as in "George Mikan and the Minneapolis Lakers vs. the New York Knickerbockers."

"They took me on my reputation," Sailors said of the Cleveland club, which was well aware he had been a two-time All-American.

Pro basketball was far from becoming the global affair it is today where players command multimillion-dollar salaries routinely. But the cost of living was much, much lower, too, and Sailors had studied that aspect of daily life before negotiating a deal.

"A new three-bedroom home in Laramie would cost you about $3,500," he said. "A haircut was thirty-five cents. The $7,500 was big money for those days. I couldn't get that playing AAU ball. Phillips 66 made me an offer. They were going to give me $4,000. They were going to give me a job, too, but I didn't want it."

Sailors had a two-pronged plan. He wanted to make enough money to take care of his family (son Dan was born in 1947) and to stockpile some to get another business going for his post-playing days. There was still some general prejudice against professionalism in sports and it so happened that Wyoming Coach Everett Shelton was one of those people who believed more strongly in amateurism and Olympic ideals then getting paid to play.

"Shelton kind of got irked at me because I didn't take that job," Sailors said of the Phillips 66 opportunity. "He didn't like the pros, either. He frowned on professionalism, which is hard to explain to people today. But I didn't really care. I wanted money. I wanted to make some money for my family. Bokie and I saved money. She was saving more than I was. We were able to buy the Heart 6 Ranch in Jackson Hole to set up our business."

That came a little bit later, but laid the groundwork for Sailors's future as an outdoors guide in Wyoming and Alaska.

Sailors's first year in pro basketball he averaged 9.9 points a game in fifty-eight games. For the first time, though, he ran into a coach who was opposed to him using his jump shot, just hated it. It was coincidental that several members of the Original Celtics had gravitated toward coaching and always crossed paths with Sailors. Joe Lapchick and Nat Holman had already seen the jump shot at work. Cleveland coach Dutch Dehnert, one of their old teammates, did not have the vision to see the jump shot as a dangerous weapon.

Sometimes Dehnert yanked Sailors from games when he employed the jumper. Sometimes he kept him on the bench so he wouldn't use the jumper. He disdained it. "You'll never go in this league with that kind of shot," Dehnert said.

The Rebels finished third in the Western Division with a 30–30 record and lost a first-round, best-two-games-out-of-three playoff series to the New York Knicks.

There was little doubt that the best basketball in the country was being played in the BAA, although not all of the best players were yet gathered under one league umbrella. The league was desperately trying to carve out a niche on the American sporting scene, trying to gain as much newspaper publicity as possible and sneak coverage into the local dailies in-between the articles about baseball, boxing, and horse racing, which were then the three most popular sports in the nation (with college football probably ranking fourth).

Most of the early basketball team owners were wealthy individuals who made their money in other fields, but who didn't have the deep pockets of the really rich businessmen that were the captains of industry and were American royalty like the Vanderbilts, Carnegies, and Rockefellers. In some instances they owned the civic arenas where their teams played and they also owned the NHL teams that accounted for the use of several dates in those buildings. Some felt basketball would be complementary to hockey, filling the empty nights in the arenas when the hockey teams were off or playing on the road.

Some of those pioneer owners were Walter Brown in Boston, Eddie Gottlieb in Philadelphia, Ned Irish in New York, and Ben Kerner, with Tri-Cities, who later moved that squad to St. Louis where it became the Hawks (who now play in Atlanta).

"It was a strange league," Sailors said. "Teams came in for a couple of months."

One thing that made Sailors saleable as a pro, more so than his jump shooting accuracy, was his dribbling skill. He was a superb ball handler and without a shot clock and no half-court, ten-second line in effect, he could dribble around as long as he wanted to if that was the team's keep-away strategy.

"Two men couldn't take the ball away from him," said Floyd Volker, the Wyoming teammate of Sailors's who also played one season in the pros with him.

The lack of a rule requiring a team to bring the ball past half-court within ten seconds was a huge aid to Sailors because it gave him more room to dribble and made it more difficult for teams to trap him.

"I dribbled out the clock," he said. "If there were more than two guys on me I'd look for the open man. You had the backcourt, you see, and it was tough to corner a guy."

Overall, the pro game was not as polished as it later became. Many times there was a windchill factor in arenas because there were so many empty seats. Travel was mostly by train, not plane. The game itself could be more violent, with harder hits when a player drove to the basket. More fights broke out than are tolerated today. It was the same sport, but a different world.

One early NBA player was Johnny Bach, who played one season with the Celtics in the 1940s before beginning a distinguished career as a college coach at Fordham and later as an assistant coach for the NBA Chicago Bulls.

"It's a different game," said Bach, who at eighty-nine is still scouting for the Bulls. "Everything is different. It just blossomed so quickly."

A 6-foot-2 guard, Bach has been a basketball insider for more than sixty-five years and marvels at how the sport has grown and matured.

"It became international," Bach said. "It went from being a small, little, old pro league into an internationally popular sport."

Bach played against Sailors in the pros and said he was a hard man to cover because of his quickness.

"What a great dribbler," Bach said. "He was a blazing fast, high-jumping guard who came into Madison Square Garden with the jump shot."

Anyone who played in the NBA in the 1940s should be looked at as a pioneer, but Bach said the current crop of players that are used to the big money, being flown between cities on private jets, and staying in luxury hotels would not believe the conditions and circumstances of pro life prior to 1950.

"For one thing you had to get a job for the summer," Bach said. "Basketball was part-time. I worked for Swift and Company, the meat company. Mostly we took trains to games, though for the short distances we took buses. There were no airplanes. Wait. I think once we flew from Boston to Chicago. The average salary was about $5,500 a year and our per diem, to cover our meals, was $7 to $9 a day."

Bach grew up in New York and played his college ball at Fordham. By 1948, when Bach was graduating, the NBA had a draft and he was chosen by the Celtics. The Sheboygan Redskins of the National Basketball League also drafted him. As a New Yorker, Boston sounded better to him than Wisconsin and he signed with the Celtics.

Another memory of Bach's, who later was head coach of the Golden State Warriors in the 1980s, that would never occur in present-day NBA hoops, was being shut out of a home court. Boston was scheduled to play the Knicks, but Madison Square Garden was unavailable, perhaps, he thinks, because of a conflict with the circus.

"They couldn't get in the Garden and we played in the Sixty-Ninth Street Armory," Bach said. "In Boston sometimes we played in the Boston Arena." The Arena was smaller than the Boston Garden, which the Bruins ruled by virtue of a more passionate fan base.

One thing the Celtics did to build fan interest was take the team on the road during the preseason to play games in other New England cities. The trips seemed to last an eternity—Bach remembers his year it being sixteen games long.

"Our training camp was a bus tour," Bach said. "There was the team, the coaches, and we rarely had a trainer (the players taped each other's ankles). Can you imagine being on the bus that long?"

Actually, in the future, for many years the Celtics played some regular-season home games in Hartford, Connecticut, and Providence, Rhode Island.

Another difference at the time was the use of just two game officials, not three, something that did not change for many years. Once, Bach recalled, one of the two officials assigned to a game could not get to the arena in time because fog held up his plane. That left one official in charge of the game—Bach was not certain of his name—who announced to the teams that his strategy was going to be to stay in one place for the entire forty-eight-minute contest.

"I'm going to stand at mid-court," he said. "If you SOBs think I'm going to run back and forth, you're nuts."

Meanwhile, when Sailors went to Cleveland to play basketball, wife Marilynne, daughter Linda, and son Dan stayed in Wyoming.

"She was mostly with my mother in Cheyenne helping her run a convalescent home for elderly people and she enjoyed that," Sailors said.

He and several of his teammates banded together and rented a house from a local resident who offered a reasonable price. They slept two to a room, just like college travel days.

"Cleveland was a pretty nice town," Sailors said. "I liked it. We were in a residential district. We enjoyed it. I wish I could have gone back there to play, but the owners lost a lot of money. The Cleveland Indians were big then, the Browns were coming on, and the Cleveland Barons hockey team was big. Otto Graham became a big hit with the Browns. I saw him play that year I was there."

At that time the Browns were members of the All-America Football Conference, an upstart competitor to the National Football League. The AAFC started in 1946, the same year as the NBA. Sailors was part of the birth of the basketball league and a spectator to the birth of the football league. Although the Browns made it big, he did note the irony that one league, the basketball one, was still going strong nearly seventy years later, while the football one was out of business in four years.

"That's something," Sailors said. "I just don't think they were tuned into basketball at that time in Cleveland."

While Dehnert denigrated the use of the jump shot, management did not endorse his general way of thinking and he did not last through the season as head man in Cleveland. He told Sailors he was going to teach him how to shoot a two-handed set shot, but before he made any move to do so he was replaced by Roy Clifford.

Sailors's Cleveland roommate was a former Seton Hall player named Ben Scharnus who recognized immediately his teammate's problem with the club. "Kenny," he said, "when you've got a coach like Dutch that doesn't like your style and he doesn't like your jump shot, there isn't much you can do." Scharnus told Sailors he had to go to management and tell officials that he couldn't play for Dehnert.

"Dutch told me my shot wouldn't go in that league and that neither would my dribble," Sailors said. "So he wouldn't start me and I wasn't getting any playing time. I didn't really know what Dutch wanted me to do. He didn't really know a lot about coaching. He was a good player when he was younger, but he just didn't know how to handle these players, these kids, right out of college."

Sailors did complain to management, and of course Dehnert got wind of it and held that against him, too.

"I liked old Dutch," Sailors said. "He was alright. But I told them, 'I can see I'm not going to play for Dutch. It's not good for you or the team. You're paying me good money and it's sure not going to be good for me. I'd like to ask for you to trade me to somebody, or sell me, that can use me. They said, 'Kenny, just sit tight.' Pretty soon, Dutch was gone. They sent him out on the road scouting."

Clifford gave Sailors more playing time and he finished second in the league in assists per game, though the figure was not impressive compared to the current level of production with the statistic since teams scored so many fewer points. Sailors averaged 2.3.

"The best thing in the world that happened to me was Clifford getting hired," Sailors said. "When he took over the team I started right off the bat. He had seen me play in the Garden and everything. He took over when we were 17–20 and we went 13–10 under him. We played better. Once we got rid of old Dutch we started winning. Dutch never played me more than six, eight, or ten minutes a game."

Once Sailors got some game action he performed well. As a point guard he had a big man in 6-foot-5 Ed Sadowski who had come to the Rebels in a trade. Sailors fed Sadowski the way he fed Milo Komenich in college. Sadowski was the fourth leading scorer in the league that year.

A third double-figure scorer for the Rebels was Mel Riebe, who scored at a

12.1 clip. "He could shoot from outside and he could drive," Sailors said. "He had a good set shot. He took two-hand set shots. Dutch was the only one who ever complained about my jump shot. He said, 'You'll never make it with that leap and one-hander.'"

However, although Sailors had grown comfortable in Cleveland, there was no second season in the BAA for the Rebels. The Cleveland Rebels folded after that year.

"I liked old Clifford," Sailors said. "Sure, I would have come back there. Clifford was a pretty good coach. He knew what it was all about. Dutch didn't know much about the modern game (1940s style). They hired him based on his history as a player. It was a whole different ball game, just like it's a different ball game now from when I played."

Sailors had signed just a one-year contract—all contracts were one-year deals then—and received a letter from the Rebels in the middle of the summer of 1947 informing him that the team had dissolved. Former Rebel players were to be distributed to other teams by lottery. Names were put in a hat at the league office in New York and drawn out by people representing the remaining teams.

"Automatically, when a team went under the players became the property of the league," Sailors said. "They didn't sell them. They just controlled them until they could have a drawing. Each owner got a chance to draw for one player and that's how I ended up in Chicago where they had absolutely no need for me."

Sailors's second season in the pros mirrored some of the upheaval that the league itself was going through.

For the second year in a row Sailors was free of team allegiance and was about to bounce around the league during the 1947–48 season more than the leather ball did. He started the season with the Chicago Stags, moved on to the Philadelphia Warriors, and ended up with the Providence Steamrollers.

"There was some three-team deal and I went to Philadelphia and Philadelphia didn't need me either," Sailors said. "They had point guards and the coaches wanted to keep their team intact that won the league the year before."

Through all of his transactions Sailors averaged 11.9 points a game that season. Whenever a coach put Sailors in the game he put points on the board. Only fifteen players scored more points per game in the league that year than Sailors. Teams were only averaging 70-something-points per game. Sailors appeared in forty-four games that year, but because of tumult in the league the schedule only called for forty-eight games, a one-time aberration.

Sailors began the year with the Stags, who featured the league's top scorer in Max Zaslofsky, a 6-foot-2 guard from New York who that season became the youngest player at twenty-one to be named first-team all-league until LeBron James after the 2005–6 season and the youngest league scoring champion until 2010 when Kevin Durant bested him. Zaslofsky, who was only fifty-nine when he died in 1985, was one of the league's first great players.

"Max was one of the best," Sailors said.

Chicago shipped Sailors to Philadelphia and there he teamed in the backcourt with Joe Fulks. Eddie Gottlieb, who really was a legendary promoter in Philadelphia, that city's Ned Irish, in essence, and one of the real pioneers of the NBA, was acting as coach at the time.

"I liked Eddie," Sailors said. "His idea of coaching was to throw the ball out on the court and give it to Fulks. There were a lot of other good players there, too. Howie Dallmar was a pretty good player [12.2 average that season]. George Senesky was quite a ballplayer and he was the point guard. He made a lot of All-American teams with me in 1943. He went to St. Joseph's University. That was a good team. Fulks was the big shot, though. I played with Fulks in the Marines in San Diego and one thing that made him great was that he was always following his shot the minute it left his hands. He was chasing that ball. I saw him recover his own shot five times and still end up making the bucket."

Fulks had carte blanche to shoot at will for the Warriors and in the league's first year he took four hundred more shots than the next busiest player. The second year he took a hundred more shots than Zaslofsky and three hundred more shots than the third most active shooter.

"Joe did get more shots," Sailors said, "and a lot of them came when he followed his own shot. He'd shoot from the free-throw line, or farther out, and if it didn't go in the basket, he'd chase it down and shoot under the basket, rebounding until he put it in."

Finally, feeling a little bit like a pinball, Sailors was shipped to Providence to finish out the 1947–48 season and he played forty-one games there. In the ever-changing world of pro basketball at least at the end of the year the Steamrollers were still in business and were going to put a team on the court again for the 1948–49 season.

"Providence was the only one of those teams that could really use me," Sailors said.

CHAPTER 10

Steamrolled Out of Providence

WHEN KENNY SAILORS STEPPED OFF THE MERRY-GO-ROUND of his 1947–48 season he was employed by the Providence Steamrollers. Providence is located about forty-five miles from Boston, which may not have been a big deal at the dawn of the pro league, but was destined to kill off the team trying to make it in the same general market as the Boston Celtics.

Providence was kinder to Sailors than Cleveland, Chicago, or Philadelphia had been. He found regular playing time and emerged as the leading scorer and playmaker for the Steamrollers that season and the next year, as well.

The biggest obstacle in Providence at the time, though, was winning. The Steamrollers finished 6–42 in the shortened '47–48 season.

"It seemed like they changed coaches every week," Sailors said. "The big issue was that we didn't have a big man. You couldn't play in that league without a big man. You had to have one. It was depressing losing all of the time. The owners wouldn't spend the money to get a big man. I was pretty disgusted by all of the losing, but I was in it for the money. That was my job. As long as I got paid I was going to stay. They didn't miss any paychecks. They paid us."

Sailors averaged 15.8 points a game and 3.7 assists per game for the 1948–49 season. He was eighth in the league in both categories and that made him popular enough in Providence to gain his first product endorsement. The top stars in pro basketball today can earn millions of dollars by lending their names to basketball shoe manufacturers, car dealerships, wireless phone companies, or food products.

However, it is unlikely that any player now, or ever, had a less glamorous endorsement deal than Sailors did with Providence. Bennett's Prune Juice did not make him rich, but he was supplied with all of the drink he wanted. The arrangement was a little less formal than it is in this era, too, without any pages-long contract.

"They didn't even ask me," Sailors said. "They just used my name and sent me cases of prune juice. The club made the money, whatever it was. Players didn't get a dime on any of that stuff. I got all the prune juice I wanted to drink, but that wasn't too much. I did drink it. It was OK."

Somehow Sailors did not swoon over the arrangement, nor did he drink the prune juice with the gusto of the endorsers who guzzle energy replacement drinks like Gatorade for their own good and the good of their bank accounts.

Longtime Detroit sportswriter Joe Falls wrote a flashback story about a play Sailors made for Providence in a game in New York against the Knickerbockers, notable to Falls because it was one of the most remarkable shots he ever saw on a court.

"Kenny Sailors had this strange habit," Falls wrote in the *Detroit Free Press*. "He would dribble across center court, head in to the top of the key and catapult high into the air. He'd hang up there as if suspended by some invisible wires and decide whether to shoot his one-hander or pass off to one of his teammates. Skinny George Nostrand was in the pivot for the Steamrollers. He was sliding in and out with his back to the basket. Sailors suddenly cut the ball loose. But poor George wasn't looking. The ball hit him on the forehead, bounced high into the air and . . . swish . . . it came down through the cords for two points!"

Now that's a flashy assist.

Sailors was a hit in Providence, and so was Ernie Calverley. Calverley was a 5-foot-10 guard who had starred for the University of Rhode Island and was famous for hitting a half-court shot to give the Rams a victory in an NIT semifinal game at Madison Square Garden. Calverley averaged 11.9 points and 2.5 assists for Providence during the 1947–48 season and 9.4 points a game the next year.

"Calverley was small, but he was a good ballplayer," Sailors said. "We didn't hit if off too well. I think he was a little jealous of me. He was my only problem in Providence. He was the big man on campus until I got there and then he had to share it with me. He didn't like that too well."

That was one of Providence's problems. Sailors and Calverley were both about the same height, which was on the small side for the pros even then, and they were both ideal at the same position. The Steamrollers finished a horrible 12–48 that year.

One of Sailors's teammates with the 1948–49 Steamrollers was a 6-foot-4, 205-pound rookie out of Miami of Ohio named Bobby Brown. Brown has fond memories of playing with Sailors in Providence, but also in Denver, and in the service, too.

"He was the innovator of the jump shot," Brown said. "The coaches were still teaching most people how to shoot the two-hand set shot. I used the two-handed shot, except when I got near the basket. Then I used a left-handed or right-handed hook. Kenny was very competitive. He used to cherry-pick a little [cheat headed downcourt for a fast break]. He was just a prince."

Brown, who was eighty-nine as he spoke about the early days of the NBA, said the most he made as a pro ballplayer was $5,000 a year, but that wasn't a bad salary at the time, either. "That's what the times were," he said.

Rarely, and only when the schedule strictly dictated it, Brown said, the early teams flew to game dates, perhaps in a DC-3. Other times they rolled by train or bus.

"We had frequent flyer miles," Brown said. "We had charters. They had four wheels."

Sometimes those four wheels weren't very luxurious. Once, Brown said, the Steamrollers played a home game on a Tuesday night, then "jumped into four or five automobiles and drove to Indiana" for a game. Then they drove to Chicago for a game against the Stags the next night, on to Minneapolis, and then to Tri-Cities.

It was difficult enough to win on the road, but harder still to win when the players never got a good night's rest.

The second season in Providence, Sailors had his entire family with him. Wife Bokie, daughter Linda, and son Dan all came east that year. It started that way, anyway. But Bokie soon was diagnosed with what became a lifetime affliction—emphysema.

"She had a lot of breathing troubles," Sailors said, "and she was a young woman then. They couldn't do much for her, so she pretty much had it all of her life. She got sick in Providence and we called her aunt, Annie Hershiser, in Casper, and she came and spent the winter with us. She was a grand old lady and she was in her seventies then. If she hadn't come we were going to go home to Wyoming."

The Sailorses drove from Wyoming in a Cadillac hauling a trailer and rented a house about twenty miles outside of Providence because they preferred the country over the city. Aunt Annie pretty much took care of everyone while Kenny played ball.

"It was a bad winter, with a lot of snow, and Marilynne just couldn't handle it," Sailors said. "I'd come home and the snowplows had just about completely covered my car. I couldn't even see it sometimes. I'd have to go probing around with a shovel. Annie saved our necks that year. I couldn't even have stayed in the league if it hadn't been for her."

The season was much shorter then, so the family sojourn in Rhode Island lasted only about four and a half months and then everyone piled back into the car and hauled that trailer back across the country to Wyoming.

Sailors tends to laugh when someone asks him what the differences are between the NBA of 2013 and the NBA of 1948 and 1949. Besides the travel by planes versus trains, besides the pay being in the millions of dollars instead of the thousands, besides the media attention and TV exposure, the addition of the 24-second clock to speed up games and the institution of the half-court ten-second line—in other words, everything.

"The play was different, too," Sailors said. "They set a lot more screens back in that day. They don't set a lot of real screens today. If you're good enough to pick your man off one of your teammates on the dribble, why it's a screen, otherwise it isn't."

Nowadays fans of an NBA team that reside in China can follow the Indiana Pacers or the Chicago Bulls on the Internet. In Sailors's day fans could not watch their team on TV, but could listen on the radio. The local newspapers did not travel to away games, but covered the home games.

Sailors, and eventually a few others, attempted jump shots. The one player Sailors remembers most clearly playing against was Belus Smawley when he played for the St. Louis Bombers, Syracuse Nationals, and Baltimore Bullets. Smawley was an early player who employed a turnaround jumper.

"Smawley was the only other one I remember shooting a jump shot when I was playing in the NBA," Sailors said. "And he didn't jump straight up. Sometimes he faded back so far he would practically fall over on his back."

Some of the earliest BAA, alias NBA teams, passed through so quickly they are not even remembered in the cities where they competed except by really old-timers. The Pittsburgh Ironmen lasted one year and although the

American Basketball Association was represented by the Pittsburgh Condors and then the Pittsburgh Pipers, there has not been a pro team in the Steel City since 1972. The Toronto Huskies long predated the Toronto Raptors, as did the Indianapolis Olympics predate the Indiana Pacers. The Detroit Pistons used to be the Fort Wayne Pistons in Indiana. The Pistons moved to Detroit after the demise of the Detroit Falcons. Franchises came and went with dizzying speed.

The NBA now has the Washington Wizards, which used to be the Baltimore Bullets, which used to be the Chicago Packers, and then the Chicago Zephyrs. (There was more than one Bullets club.) The Washington Capitals, an early league squad, has nothing to do with the Wizards, but did give the legendary Boston Celtics coach Red Auerbach his start in the league.

"They didn't draw," Sailors said of the Capitals, which is now the name of the DC NHL team. "They didn't make money. Teams were into it to make money and they weren't making money."

There was no TV money and if attendance was low teams were doomed. At the end of the better part of Sailors's two seasons with the Steamrollers the Providence franchise was no more. Owner Lou Perini, who was a Boston businessman anyway, agreed to give up the team and become a minority owner of the Celtics instead of competing with them. Perini made his money in construction and also owned the Boston Braves baseball team starting in 1945. He was the one who moved the Braves to Milwaukee and he presided over their pennant-winning success in the Midwest through 1961 before selling the team.

More conveniently for a guy who considered Wyoming home, Sailors landed with the Denver Nuggets for the 1949–50 season. It was his best year in the pros, too, and he received All-Star recognition. That year Sailors averaged 17.3 points a game, fourth best in the league, and 4.0 assists per game. But the Nuggets were a terrible team on the court, finishing 11–51 for last place in the Western Division, eight games behind the second-to-last club.

Jack Cotton, eighty-nine, of Alamosa, Colorado, played his only season of pro ball that year, averaging 5.1 points a game, but remained friends with Sailors over the ensuing decades.

"We were the first major-league team in any sport west of the Mississippi," Cotton said. "There was no football or baseball, or anything."

He overlooked the Los Angeles Dons of the All-America Football Conference, but otherwise the farthest west team in Major League baseball was the St. Louis Cardinals, and hockey was in its Original Six era, with the Chicago Blackhawks being the farthest west team.

Cotton cites another way that the early NBA differed from the modern NBA—the width of the foul lane. Originally, it was just six feet wide and now it is twelve feet wide. Allow a player like George Mikan to roam free in that narrow space and it was impossible to guard him, Cotton said.

"His shoulders were as wide as the lane," Cotton said. "He would muscle me around and I complained when they called the foul on me. The referee would say of the fans, 'They came to watch Big George, not you.'"

Cotton got out of the US Navy in 1946. He spent one year playing at Wyoming and then felt he needed to make some money. He shared time on a barnstorming team with Sailors as they played exhibitions in small towns in Wyoming. Then he joined the Nuggets for that somewhat ill-fated season because he was married and needed to get a job. The Nuggets paid him $3,800.

"That would be meal money in the NBA now," Cotton said. "They make more in one game than I made in a season. I loved it, though."

Even if in some ways the NBA was still kind of a bush league. Cotton remembers the Fort Wayne Pistons playing at a local high school gym. He remembers Morris Udall, who later spent thirty years in the House of Representatives for Arizona, playing with vision in just one eye but playing well enough that some sportswriters felt he must have had two good eyes.

"Mo was always my bridge partner," Cotton said when they both shared the court with Denver. "We sometimes flew around on an old DC-3, though one time it broke down in Chicago."

Later, when Cotton met Udall's son Mark, he told him, "I introduced your mother to your dad." They were playing cards on a flight and Cotton thought he could make a good match for Udall with a flight attendant. "I threw down the cards and introduced her," he said.

When the team took the train to away games, the big men—Cotton was 6-foot-7—were bundled into berths together and "slept feet to feet," Cotton said.

Professional basketball did not seem like a big-time profession during those long rides trying to catch forty winks. Cotton later returned to school, earned a PhD, and for several years coached the Adams State basketball team in Colorado.

Cotton and Sailors remain in touch with periodic phone calls and have seen each other at various times over the years. Cotton said of Marilynne, "I just loved his sweetie pie. I once chopped wood for her."

Kenny as a member of the Denver Nuggets in the new NBA, 1949–50 season. (Photo courtesy the University of Wyoming.)

Cotton was a two-hand set shooter, unlike Sailors.

"It was not anything like that shot Kenny had," Cotton said. "I took some one-hand set shots and hooks. Kenny was a great jump shooter. He helped develop the jump shot. He had that jump shot right down pat. He was a good defensive player, too." Cotton admired the quickness of Sailors's hands and his quick reflexes. "I can still see Kenny walking around the hotel lobby with five silver dollars and he could throw them up in the air and catch them before they hit the ground."

The dreadful Nuggets folded after Sailors's lone All-Star season with them. At that point Sailors had completed four seasons of professional basketball and played for three teams that had gone out of business. Denver, of course, came back after a stint in the American Basketball Association in the 1960s and 1970s, and used the same nickname of Nuggets when the NBA and ABA merged.

If you were Kenny Sailors, at that point it was hard to think of playing pro basketball as very secure work. He would have been happy to play longer in Providence, if he could have.

"I had good years there in Providence," Sailors said many years later to a reporter reviewing the brief history of the Steamrollers. "We just never had a big man and you had to have a big man."

Pretty soon Providence had no men. Another team bit the dust. The players even discussed the notion that one day they would wake up and the entire league would implode, putting them all out of jobs.

"We thought about it," Sailors said of the rough times the league underwent. "But some of the old owners of ball teams were pretty organized. They were the ones who held things together. Other teams were pretty sketchy. I was making less money with Providence than I was making when I came into the league with Cleveland. They cut me a thousand dollars to $6,500."

Another prominent basketball figure that Sailors overlapped with in Denver with the Nuggets was Duane Klueh. Klueh was born in North Dakota in 1926 and played guard for Indiana State between 1946 and 1949, barely competing in college at all when Sailors was playing for Wyoming.

Klueh was a major star, winning the college basketball player of the year award from the Helms Foundation in 1948 and the Chuck Taylor Most Valuable Player award, as well. He was drafted by the Boston Celtics, but played his two NBA seasons for other teams, the Nuggets during that forty-games-under-.500 season and the Fort Wayne Pistons. He later became the longtime coach at his alma mater and won more than 60 percent of his games at Indiana State.

Sharing part of the Denver season ordeal with Sailors, Klueh remembered the Nuggets being ill-stocked with enough solid players to compete with the best teams in the league, especially after the BAA and the NBL merged.

"We played at the Denver University Field House," Klueh said. "We didn't have many really good athletes. A lot was happening with the league. This was two months after the merger. It was the beginning in every which way. But you felt like what you were doing was something fun for a while. A teacher was making $2,700 a year and when I got traded to Fort Wayne they were paying $5,500 to $5,700 a year. They were one of the Cadillac teams."

Klueh originally had no plans to play professionally at all. He already had designs on a coaching career and even had a job offer. He said one of the Denver officials cajoled him into playing.

"If it hadn't been for a pretty smooth talker out there, and he really didn't have to do that much talking, I was going to be the coach at Rockhurst College,"

Klueh said. "I enjoyed it [playing in the pros]. I met some really good people. I'd never regret it."

Sailors was one of those people that Klueh met and never forgot.

"Kenny was very unusual because of his ability to jump in the air and shoot," said Klueh, who won 182 games coaching at Indiana State later in the 1950s and well into the 1960s. "I'm sure he was much more similar to the 1960s and 1970s jump shooters than anyone else from his time."

Sometimes at practice, Klueh and others on the Nuggets might play the age-old game of 21 against Sailors. In one-on-one play the first to score that many baskets wins. That was the same game Sailors played against Bud in the backyard way back when. However, special rules were called for in Denver.

"I'd say, 'Alright, I'm going to play Kenny,'" Klueh said, "'but he has to stay on the ground.' He was a deadly shooter. I've never known anyone with the balance he had. He made the one-hander, but I was on the floor."

There were times travel for the Nuggets bordered on the absurd. There were teams just down the road from one another in Boston and New York and in Syracuse and Rochester, but no other team was located anywhere near the Nuggets. It would seem that flight was called for on occasions when driving was reality.

"It wasn't pretty," Klueh said of his most memorable road trip during a winter when the Nuggets fulfilled their schedule obligation by automobile at a time when the Interstate system had yet to be built. "We left Denver at midnight after a ball game and drove all night in three cars to Indianapolis. The car I was in was a convertible and it was cold."

About noon the next day the Nuggets arrived in Terre Haute, Klueh's hometown, where his mother greeted them with a fried chicken dinner. They drove the last stretch to Indianapolis and went right to sleep and then played that night against the Indianapolis Olympics at the Butler Fieldhouse.

"Immediately after the game we took off for a game against the Minneapolis Lakers in Rochester, and it started to sleet," Klueh said. "All three cars were in ice all the way. It took forever. I think we had breakfast in Hammond, Indiana. It took us seven hours in ice and snow in our own cars. We were still thirty-five miles away when it was time for the game to start."

That was not the end of the journey. On they went for a game against Tri-Cities on a Sunday afternoon after the Saturday night game against the Lakers.

"We hadn't been to bed yet when we reached Moline," Klueh said. "We played that game without sleep. Then we drove back to Denver. When I got there my wife said I looked like death warmed over. Maybe we had twelve to fifteen hours of sleep between Wednesday and Monday."

With those kinds of travel conditions, imposed basically because management wanted to save money, it certainly could be conceded that was a between-the-lines reason why the Nuggets finished 11–51.

"We never had any rest, never had any recovery time," Sailors said. "I remember when we came back to Denver from our first trip we only had four guys who were really healthy enough to play. We had those cars because I don't think the train even went all of the way to Rochester from Denver. Boy, oh boy. We were crippled up, guys were sick to their stomachs, everything you could ask for. It was a tough situation. I seemed to make out as well as any of them and I was the oldest guy on the ball club.

"I never played with a winner in the NBA. We were always just mediocre or the worst team in the league and that didn't help me any."

Sailors definitely played with some of the weaker teams in the league, but he did get to see the first NBA dynasty Minneapolis Lakers up close and personal. "They were the best," he said.

The Lakers won their first crown during the 1947–48 season and won four more titles by the 1953–54 season. Pivot man George Mikan was the main reason why the Lakers were unstoppable, but they were blessed with several other stars, too, including forwards Jim Pollard and Vern Mikkelsen and guard Slater Martin.

"They had the big man and tremendous forwards and guards," Sailors said. "You didn't find any better players. Mikan did most of their scoring. Pollard was also a great player. I played with him one year in AAU ball."

Pollard played for Stanford's 1942 NCAA championship team, won the five titles with the Lakers, and was a four-time All-Star before being inducted into the Naismith Basketball Hall of Fame.

"I got to know Pollard pretty well and he was a great ballplayer," Sailors said. "He told me a story about one time the Lakers were in the playoffs and they weren't doing too well. They were behind and had been for most of the game. Mikan called timeout himself and he called the team together on the court, not even over at the bench. Pollard said that Mikan went, 'Now guys, it's like this. You want to be a big shot. You want to get your name in the paper, or you want to be the star. It's fine with me. I'm going to get my money either way. But if you want to get to the finals and win the championship, throw the ball into Big George.' That's what he said—to throw the ball to him if you want to win the championship. And they did. He was right and the coach [John Kundla] knew he was right. So you couldn't argue with him."

Yet Mikan also sometimes led the championship teams in assists. He understood that if he was double-teamed that the best play was to flip the ball back out to the perimeter for one of the outside shooters.

"He'd throw it back out, you betcha," Sailors said. "Oh, Mikan could dominate. There wasn't anyone in the league that could come close to him."

The Lakers also had the capacity to reload. One of the later arrivals in the dynasty was 6-foot-9 high-powered scorer Clyde Lovellette, who had been an All-American at Kansas and an Olympic gold medal–winner and was later a Hall of Famer, too. Lovellette, who played for Phillips 66 for a year, and then at the tail end of his career won championships with the Celtics as Bill Russell's backup, currently lives in Indiana, where he grew up. Like all of the players who lived to see the evolution, he still can't get over the changes between the early NBA and the modern NBA.

"You mostly bused it or trained it," Lovellette said. "The Fort Wayne Pistons had their own plane that the owner, Fred Zollner, had, and in those days, which people don't remember much, the NBA scheduled doubleheaders. There would be one game with two visiting teams and the second game would feature the home team. So sometimes you would play the Pistons at their home and then travel to the same city for part of a doubleheader. They might invite you to join them on the plane and travel together. It wasn't until the late 1950s and early 1960s when we started flying commercial, especially after Los Angeles and San Francisco came into the league."

Lovellette played on the final Minneapolis title team with Mikan and he said the veteran taught him a lot of tricks in terms of battling in the low post where there was considerable contact.

"I won the last championship with the Lakers," Lovellette said. "George was in his twilight. It was sort of going out in style. George was a tremendous mentor to me, teaching me to survive. It was a little rougher than it is now."

Many teams employed an enforcer, a designated tough guy who was supposed to police the opposition and keep the other team's strong men away from his team's star. This was much like what has long been the case in hockey.

"If there was a fight it didn't last long," Lovellette said, "but the fine was $50 or $100. That doesn't sound like much, but it was a lot of money then. The old-timers, I think we really enjoyed playing basketball. We were more of a family. We had more time away from the court together than they do now."

By the time Lovellette turned pro the shakedown of teams had taken place and during his career there were eight clubs in the NBA. Salaries had gone up, too, and he made $15,000 a year when he started. He also did better than Sailors in the endorsement business, having deals that paid him for putting his stamp of approval on Spalding basketballs and Ford automobiles.

Lovellette just missed being in the league with Sailors. He was of the next generation and because he had a long pro career he went head-to-head regularly with all-time superstars Wilt Chamberlain and Bill Russell (before he joined the Celtics).

"I enjoyed playing against Wilt," Lovellette said. "Most guys would cringe when they had to go up against a player like him. I took him outside. He didn't want to cover me there. Inside, he was a really strong individual. But I'd pick Russell over Chamberlain for reboundimg, defense, and teamwork."

One of the other fine early NBA teams that won a championship, interrupting the Lakers' run, was the Rochester Royals. The average fan doesn't even know that the Rochester Royals ever existed, but the team that won the 1950–51 title is the linear forebearer of the Sacramento Kings. Over the years the Rochester Royals became the Cincinnati Royals and then became the Kansas City–Omaha Kings, splitting time between the two cities before sticking to Kansas City for a while. The franchise relocated to Sacramento in 1985.

"Fans wouldn't know what you were talking about, but they had a great team," Sailors said of Rochester, the club he nearly joined. "They had two great guards in Bob Davies and Bob Wanzer, and Arnie Risen was a good player. They also had Red Holzman, who later coached the Knicks."

Following the same pattern as he had experienced before, Sailors found himself without a team after the 1949–50 season. The Nuggets went out of business and there he was, once again, an unemployed pro basketball player. This time when his name was drawn out of an upside-down fedora, he belonged to the Boston Celtics.

Whenever he got decent playing time Sailors was a success. He said he knew he had to score to thrive in the league.

"It didn't take me too long to figure it out," he said. "If I didn't end up in the top ten in scoring in the league they were going to cut my salary and the next team that got me was going to cut my salary. If they did, I was probably going to leave the league and go home to Wyoming. I had the attitude, 'I have to score to stay in this league.'"

There was nothing wrong with being a member of the Celtics, although this was several years before the team, under Red Auerbach, became the greatest sports dynasty of all time by winning eleven world championships in thirteen seasons. The Celtics of 1950–51 were not that caliber of team yet, however.

For that matter, Auerbach was not yet the famed coach he would become. By that season Auerbach had coached the Washington Capitals for three seasons (including a 49–11 best record in the inaugural year of the league) and the Tri-Cities Blackhawks for one year. The 1950–51 campaign was Auerbach's first in Boston.

One thing the Celtics did not need, though, was a 5-foot-11 point guard. They already had Bob Cousy, the former Holy Cross All-American who was revered in New England. Cousy, who introduced the behind-the-back pass to the pro game, was not going to be budged out of the playmaking guard role, so once again Sailors found himself playing for a team that didn't really need him. Still, at least the Celtics weren't going to fold in the next ten minutes.

"There wasn't much job security the way teams I played on kept going out of business," Sailors said. "The only way I kept at it was being a high scorer and my assists."

Sailors was dizzy from his own comings and goings in the league and the teams' coming and goings. He laughed when asked how a young fan of today would react upon learning that the NBA once had teams in Anderson, Indiana, or Waterloo, Iowa.

"How about Tri-Cities?" he said. "Poor Red Auerbach. When the Capitals gave it up he ended up in Tri-Cities for a year working with Ben Kerner. They didn't get along. When I got to the Celtics he told me once, 'I hate that place. I hate it.' He was happy to go back to the East Coast with the Celtics. Red was alright. I liked Red, though he did some things that I didn't like. He'd light up that cigar at the end of every game that he won. There was no smoking and there were little kids everywhere and he would be, 'I'm Red Auerbach. I can smoke.' And he'd blow the smoke towards you when they clinched a win. I didn't like that. He was acting like a big kid, doing something that a fifteen-or-sixteen-year-old kid would do."

Auerbach really was a young coach when Sailors joined the Celtics—he was just thirty-three when the season started. At the time he was viewed as just another coach, but eventually he came to be regarded as one of the greatest coaches who ever lived, who helped spread the popularity of the sport to Europe by giving clinics, although Sailors had some reservations.

"He was a tremendous judge of talent, but as far as his real knowledge of the game, I don't know," Sailors said. "I never thought of him as a great coach who had knowledge of the science and tactics of the game, but he knew how to get the best out of his ballplayers. There was something about that guy. He could sign up these ballplayers and get great ones. Red was alright and a bit of a character."

Once again, though, Sailors knew he had ended up with a team that didn't really have a strong need for him. Ironically, one player Auerbach nearly whiffed on as a talent evaluator was Bob Cousy, the Hall of Fame guard. Auerbach was trying to establish himself in Boston and he did not want a player on the team who was more popular than he was from the get-go.

"He figured that Cousy had a great reputation there in Boston," Sailors said. "He didn't want anyone to be bigger than him."

Cousy did eclipse Auerbach's popularity with his achievements, but the two ended up becoming very close. Cousy was the only person in the world besides Mrs. Auerbach who referred to Red by his given name of Arnold.

Sailors reported to Boston in time for the 1950–51 exhibition season, but made a quick visit to team owner Walter Brown.

"Walter Brown knew that I was a good ballplayer and had done well in Providence for Lou Perini," Sailors said. "I told him I wasn't sure I could play for Red and I felt that deep down Red didn't want me because he had a lot of talent in my category. 'He doesn't have any real need for me. I'd really appreciate it if you could make some kind of deal with Baltimore. The Bullets told me they'd like to have me.'"

Time passed. Sailors did stay with the Celtics through the exhibition season and into the regular season and got some playing time. That was the season the NBA was integrated by three African-American players virtually simultaneously. Chuck Cooper out of Duquesne was the first black player drafted by the NBA when the Celtics took him. The story goes that when Walter Brown announced his pick there was a hush in the room filled with other owners, then one cleared his throat and tentatively asked if Brown knew that Cooper was an African-American. Brown famously replied that he didn't care if he was polka dot.

Minutes later the Washington Capitols drafted Earl Lloyd out of West Virginia State. Lloyd actually was the first African-American to appear in an NBA game later that season. Nat "Sweetwater" Clifton had been playing for the Harlem Globetrotters when the Knicks signed him. He made his NBA debut four days after Lloyd.

Sailors got to know Cooper—they roomed together part of the time—and was amazed at the prejudicial conduct he endured because of his black skin.

"It was pitiful," Sailors said. "They wouldn't let him stay in the same places as us. When I'd say something about it, he said, 'Ah, Sailors, it'll shape up. Give it time.' I wanted to room with him to talk with him about blacks in the league. He was a nice guy. We roomed together during the exhibition season when we were in Maine and New Hampshire. The fans seemed to treat him alright. He wasn't a great ballplayer, but he was good. We mostly talked about opportunities in the league for blacks. He said, 'It'll work out. It's going to take a while. It's not going to come overnight.'"

Cooper played with Boston between 1950 and 1954 and stayed in the league through 1956. His lifetime points average was 6.7.

On a trip to Chicago, when the Celtics arrived, the hotel they were scheduled to stay at refused to admit Cooper. "Auerbach said, 'Well, the team's not going to stay here if you won't let all of our team stay here,'" Sailors recalled. "They said something like, 'We don't have anything to do with it. We've been told we can't take blacks, so that's it.' I was Cooper's roommate at the time and we went to him and said, 'What happens when you can't stay with us?' He said, 'Kenny, I do much better. The team has to give me money for a room and I get some money for extras that you don't get. I'm not mad about it at all. I make a lot of extra money when this happens.' He said he went into the colored district and everyone there took care of him for nothing. He said he stayed in Harlem in New York and the black district in Chicago."

Cousy, who became a member of the NAACP, although he was white, befriended Cooper and although he recognized the discrimination said the breakthrough of blacks in the NBA produced very little attention compared to Jackie Robinson's integration of Major League Baseball in 1947 with the Brooklyn Dodgers.

"It went virtually unnoticed," Cousy said. "And this was a few years after Jackie Robinson broke in. When the NBA integrated it got almost nothing whatsoever in terms of attention, but that's basically because of where the sport was. It was at the bottom."

"Nice guy, but he wasn't a great coach," Sailors said.

If anything, the NBA in the 1950s got a little rougher than it had been during the 1940s until the commissioner's office began cracking down. Sailors, who was hardly the biggest player on his teams, was used to getting clobbered with elbows and body blocks when he drove to the hoop and the big men shifted onto him.

"I had black and blue spots, but I expected there to be contact," he said. "They didn't call a lot of stuff back then, but it didn't bother me. I was used to it."

Although Sailors was stuck on another losing team the Bullets did have an unusual personnel situation. One member of the team was Sailors, who had popularized the standard jump shot, and another was Belus Smawley, who had been perfecting his own kind of jump shot with his fallaway. Baltimore was the only team in the league that had two players who shot jump shots, even if they were distinctive in style and approach.

"I would say he had a jump shot of a fashion," Sailors said. "It wasn't anything like mine. It was queer, one of the strangest shots I ever saw. In fact, he'd go back so far sometimes he'd fall over backwards. But he'd always release the ball before he hit the floor. He was quite a ballplayer and he became a good friend of mine when we played in Baltimore."

Smawley played forty-four games for Baltimore that year and was the Bullets' leading scorer with a 13.8-point average. He also averaged 2.8 assists a game.

One of the key reasons why Sailors played professional basketball was for the money. It represented his best chance to get ahead in life a little bit. He never made more than the $7,500 he earned his first year and he was making around $6,500 after five years in the league. A few years later players who stuck with it might have been making $25,000 or $33,000 a year.

Sailors had planned to play five seasons and then retire, though if he was a $3-million-a-year man now and he was thirty years old he probably wouldn't have quit. Playing five years, Sailors figured, would give him a pension some day.

"I had my years in," he said. "I told my wife, 'Honey, I'll be home as soon as I get my five years in. I didn't want to play anymore. I wanted to go back to my family. I had been overseas during World War II, for crying out loud, and I had been playing five years of pro ball mostly separated from them. I wanted to be back in my home with my wife and my children. It meant more to me to go back to Wyoming with them."

Five years of professional basketball seemed like plenty to Sailors at the time. It wasn't as glamorous or enriching a life as it later became. The prestige was limited, though there is more reflected glory in retrospect if Sailors tells someone that he played the first five years of the NBA.

He didn't enjoy having teams fold under him repeatedly, or being benched by coaches if they didn't like his jump shot, or watch playing time being given to others he felt were not as talented. He has speculated that if he hadn't been older and more mature when he came into the pros after serving in the military he might not have had any patience to put up with all the moving around.

"I had a lot of things going for me and I had a lot of things against me," Sailors said. "Being older helped me a lot playing in the NBA. A lot of younger boys would not have had the patience to go through what I did and kept going. They'd have gone home if Dutch Dehnert wouldn't let them play because of how they shot."

When Sailors started seriously thinking about retiring from playing basketball, some college teams expressed interest in him as an assistant coach. He heard from Iowa State, Portland State, and maybe another place or two. His old coach, Everett Shelton, asked him if he would like to coach the freshman team at Wyoming, his alma mater. Sailors rejected all such feelers.

"I didn't want to coach," Sailors said. "I was old enough to know that you had to win or you were gone. If you didn't win by three years you had to start thinking about getting out. It never intrigued me at all to try coaching at the college level. I had people putting my name in for jobs when they knew they were going to be vacant."

Sailors had zero interest in coaching, but a lot of interest in going into a new field. He wanted to be a hunting guide and Wyoming was one of the best places in the United States to do it.

Wyoming is one of the nation's small number of hunting paradises, a place of rugged and remote country, dotted with mountains. It is a rural state where most of the cities are small and big game abounds not far from the doorstep. Kenny and Marilynne had the outdoors in their blood and they wanted to make their living in the outdoors. Sailors had a big name in Wyoming from his basketball career and being the captain of the 1943 NCAA championship team, so he thought that might translate into business as a guide.

In the off-seasons during his NBA playing days Sailors eased into the lifestyle that would become his permanent profession once he stopped dribbling and jumping in the air with a ball. He and Bokie managed a lodge—the Jackson

A family photo taken in Cheyenne, Wyoming, of Kenny and Marilynne with their children Linda (left) and Dan (right). The photo was taken in January 1952 by Kenny's father-in-law, B. H. Corbin. (Photo courtesy Kenny Sailors.)

Lake Lodge—that was owned by Nelson Rockefeller and his family and later became part of the Teton National Forest.

"It was a tremendous log building," Sailors said. "It was not that big monstrosity that they've got there now for a lodge, which looks like a mental institution. It was the old lodge, a beautiful place. There were three or four walk-in fireplaces. On Saturday nights they had big dances there and we could probably feed two hundred people in the dining room. Governor Nels Smith helped us get the job. It was a big operation." Until then neither Sailors nor Bokie had spent any time in Jackson Hole, but they found that they liked it and once that happened they went on the prowl for their own land.

"We located this old Mormon couple—he went by Dad Turner," Sailors said, "and they wanted to retire, so we bought them out. That was the Heart 6 Ranch. We paid them $45,000. A long time later I saw that it sold for $13 million. It was a nice place before we got it, but we started building modern cabins and added on to the lodge. We had twenty-three hundred acres of leased land from the Forest Service used for pasture for the horses and eighty acres of deeded land. Our two kids grew up there, went to school there in a little place called Moran. It was a one-room schoolhouse with a wooden stove in the corner in the wintertime. My wife was chairman of the school board. When the kids got to the eighth grade they were bused into Jackson."

The Sailors family lived on that property for nineteen years. It was in Jackson Hole that Sailors set up his hunting guide business and he and Bokie operated a dude ranch. He actually got the business going while he was still active and he was planning for his future beyond basketball.

"I wanted to get into the guiding and outfitting business," Sailors said. And he wanted security beyond what basketball seemed prepared to offer with teams folding each year, or his being traded from town to town. "I always had my hunting to fall back on to make a living."

Although ironically Sailors is best known for what he accomplished in a sport that is played indoors he always wanted to be a professional outdoorsman. He was often seen wearing a cowboy hat—and for many years, the same cowboy hat. If he had been born in another century Sailors would surely have been a cowboy. The best he could do in the twentieth century was play sports as a Cowboy.

Wyoming has some high country, with mountains taller than thirteen thousand feet, and one of the species coveted by hunters is sheep, which tend to stay high above sea level. The other most sought-after species in Wyoming is elk. It helps to be in good athletic condition or hunting shape because the hunts usually require long hikes over steep and sometimes treacherous terrain and in gradually thinning air as the human ascends.

"A hunter who wants a sheep mount for his wall is going to work for it because sheep inhabit the high country," Sailors said. "And when you're in the high country the air is thin and tough on the lungs, and the weather is more liable to be tough on your body. The cold, rain, and snow comes easier, stays longer, and hits you harder in the high country."

Sailors left out "earlier" in his description of the weather since foul, wintry conditions might well strike in August. Wyoming is also a very windy state, so the powerful blows can affect a hunt, as well.

"You have to be in outstanding shape to go after big game," he said. "Otherwise you won't find it. And otherwise your heart will be pounding too hard to pull the trigger when you do. I've been in excellent shape my whole life. I've just taken care of myself. Of course, basketball had something to do with that, too. You can't expect to run up and down the court for a whole game if you're overweight and out of shape. But the basketball put me in the kind of shape I needed to guide hunters in the hills."

To the best of Sailors's recollection the first guided hunts he led were in 1949. His Aunt Hattie owned a lodge in the Snowy Mountains outside of Laramie and he worked out of there briefly. Sailors had learned how to ride horses as a boy in Hillsdale and his first mount was named Paint. Hunting Wyoming's backcountry often necessitated the use of horses to reach hunting camp and Sailors loved that part of the job.

One of the first customers Sailors ever guided was after mule deer and apparently wasn't very experienced. He also had very poor vision and Sailors and his wife referred to him as their "blind hunter." Bokie listened to Sailors's account of the trip and joked that he hid in the weeds so he wouldn't get shot.

Sailors and his man were in mountainous country that had little timber. Sailors deposited the hunter in a certain spot with instructions to stay put. He climbed to a higher ridge and said he would spot for game and then try to drive the game past the hunter. Sailors began hiking upward, but after about ten minutes, before he reached his destination, he heard gunshots, several gunshots. The Savage rifle the man was using only had six or eight bullets, Sailors thought, so he wondered what all of the commotion was. He thought for a minute his client had been attacked by a bear and had to fight it off in self-defense.

Sailors raced down the hillside to the hunter and came upon him pointing the rifle in one direction and firing and then repeating the move. There was no animal in sight.

"He shot up all his ammunition or else he'd still be shooting, I guess," Sailors said.

Sailors decided to sneak up on the man as if he was stalking an animal himself. He didn't want to spook him, but engulf him. When he got the man's attention he was all excited about the deer that had passed by. He was sure he had shot several of them. This would have been bad news since he only had a tag for one, but it turned out that if there had been deer in the area, he missed them all.

"He never hit a thing," Sailors said. "We walked all over the area and there was no dead deer. It was dark, though, so we came back the next day and walked all over again and never found a thing. I guess right after I left him this little bunch of deer had come down the ridge and gone past him and he just started shooting at everything that moved. He's the worst hunter I've ever had. The only thing he shot was his shadow. You bet he scared me."

That man had wanted to take a hunting trip in the wilds for years, but he had no idea what he was doing. Sailors said he didn't mind taking beginners out who had always dreamed of taking a guided hunt and saved money for years in order to be able to afford it, but it was always better if they actually told him they were beginners and listened to his advice in the field.

"Some guys are romantics," he said. "They've read a lot about hunting, read adventure stories, and have built up these fantasies over the years about how it will be."

Another time two hunters came to Jackson Hole from Chicago for a guided hunt that involved horseback riding to camp in the hills. One of the men was triple-X sized and didn't have much stamina. He weighed so much he also drained the stamina of the horse. Even after he got to camp he wanted to rest for a day or two, but when he got the itch to start hunting he didn't want to ride.

Sailors set him up on a perch where he could see for a great distance and sat him down. The guide knew an old elk buck was in the area and it might work out that it would wander past the man. Sailors worked his way down the hill with thoughts of driving the elk near his hunter. Only a short while passed before he heard a shot, a single shot. He thought it was kind of soon for the man to see any game, but he promptly reversed field and climbed back up to him.

"I shot one," the man said immediately.

Sailors told him he would scour the area and take a look. He descended to the edge of a nearby meadow only to discover the man had shot one of the party's horses.

"The worst part was that it was my daughter Linda's horse," Sailors said.

The man spent the rest of the day sobbing in his tent, apologetic, and offering to pay for the horse. Sailors assured him things would be OK. "Just be thankful it wasn't a human being," he told him. "That's the only horse we had killed on one of our hunts. He had seen the brown leg, you know. I suppose he had seen something move more than anything else."

Sailors learned pretty early during his guiding career that not everyone who joined him with a loaded weapon was a seasoned hunter and had hunted big game in Africa or the like, though many had. Ever since he tried to make sure he could gauge the experience level of hunters who signed up with him and also tried to work with them to make sure their guns were zeroed in.

"The first principle of good shooting is to get yourself in position," Sailors said. "Either sit down with your elbows on your knees, or preferably, even lie down, prone if it's possible. Hold your gun in a steady position. If I see an animal I want to shoot for meat or a trophy, I'll try to find a tree and put my rifle over a limb, or a rock, and brace up against it. Sometimes you don't have a choice, though."

It is Sailors's belief that hunters who start young should work their way into bigger caliber guns from a .22 and above all should practice a lot. He found that hunters did not shoot enough before going on a trip. Just like practicing shooting a basketball he feels it is important to shoot a rifle frequently to ensure good aim in the field when the clock is ticking down just the way it would in a ball game.

"They [hunters] just go out and practice a little bit before their local hunting season," he said, "and as a result, they tend to flinch when they shoot a big-game rifle. You have to hold steady and squeeze that trigger gently."

One of the most popular hunts in Wyoming was elk hunting season. In Wisconsin, Michigan, Illinois, Texas, and some other states, more than 100,000 deer are killed during fall seasons for that species. In Wyoming, the big-game animal pursued is the elk. In-state residents prize the meat and out-of-state residents prize the thrill of the hunt and the opportunity to chase an animal few encounter in the wild in other places.

It has been said that when hunters take off from work to chase deer in Michigan, the state has the equivalent of one of the largest armies in the world. Sailors said the elk hunting season in Wyoming was "a mob scene. It looked more like the pictures you'd see in movies when they were overthrowing the czar in Russia than any kind of hunt you could imagine."

Wyoming's elk hunting season in the 1950s when Sailors was guiding was split into two periods. The first one, starting in September, lured trophy hunters from other places while the second one was residents-only whose primary goal was more to put meat in the freezer for the winter.

It so happened that the Heart 6 Ranch was located right on the elk migration route. Sailors definitely had mixed emotions about that. As a guide it was good for business. As a local resident, he said he dreaded it because so many people flooded the area and were shooting off rifles. He only lost one horse to a stray bullet on a hunt, but more than one horse was killed when it was on his property from errant shots during elk season.

The Buffalo River was right next to the ranch and the elk crossed it by the thousands as they came out of the hills and moved to winter grounds. When word got out that the elk were on the move, so were the hunters. They checked out of work in the cities and poured into the area. One year, Sailors said, as he was returning to the ranch by horse on a cool evening at seventy-two hundred feet of altitude, he gazed upon an amazing sight.

"It looked like as far as you could see were cars, bumper to bumper," he said. "It was cars with hunters setting there and holding their guns, watching to see if the elk would cross the road. The cars were running, heaters on. You could see the exhaust coming out. Some of them brought their whole families. We had every room filled. Bokie and I together served 120 people for breakfast one morning, pancakes, ham, bacon and eggs."

People threw down bedrolls in the basement and in the barn. Cabins were filled to bursting. People slept on the living room floor and in the kitchen when it wasn't mealtime. Hunters pitched tents.

"You couldn't really call it hunting, not the way I define the sport," Sailors said.

He awoke at 4 AM, just about first light and looking out the window of the lodge Sailors saw an elk leap a fence in his pasture. A moment later a man clad in red pajamas began shouting, "The elk are here! The elk are here!"

It was like Paul Revere announcing the arrival of the British. The anxious hunters poured into the open only partially dressed, or dressing as they ran. Some were shooting as they ran.

"We were lucky nobody got shot that day," Sailors said. "It was a miracle. It would have been so easy to kill another hunter. There were these three hunters, but they all claimed they'd killed the same elk." The Fish and Game warden played the role of Solomon and made all three men share the same elk, punching all three of their tags.

Although Sailors said he and his wife found this type of gang hunting to be distasteful, he was running a business that capitalized on the crowds. He hated it when elk that were shot were not truly harvested for their meat and in the confusion were left to rot, or some hunters failed to follow up tracking wounded animals and left them crippled.

"You don't need anything to hunt this way but an elk tag and a pair of tennis shoes," Sailors said.

Around Jackson Hole, with the high altitude, it often snowed early and the elk were highlighted running over the snow. Sometimes after the passage of a herd, Sailors went out to gaze at the snow and saw puddles of blood from the animals killed. The entire scene where hunters simply stood by the side of the road and fired into the passing herd for him recalled the images of the 1800s when men slaughtered the buffalo herds in the West. But this was a government sanctioned hunt for residents.

"It was a sobering sight," Sailors said. "But the state government said this was part of their game management plan. Hunting during the migration was a way to thin the herd."

CHAPTER 12

Hunting Wyoming's Wild Country

KENNY SAILORS'S INTRODUCTION TO BEARS was in the Wyoming wild where black bears roamed amidst the other wildlife. Despite encounters with all types of animals over the years, including grizzly bears in Alaska, Sailors said that black bears are about the most unpredictable beast he has run across.

When he began guiding in Wyoming it was legal to lure black bears to hunters by using bait, though that practice has been discontinued in most places since. Although black bears are smaller than grizzly bears, they don't always scare as easily and they have claws that can be just as sharp.

Black bears don't always run away when people approach making loud noises, as they are taught to do. They seem to have a more developed sense of curiosity than grizzly bears. Historically, in the United States, the average citizen was poorly educated about black bear behavior and interaction with black bears was even encouraged at Yellowstone National Park in the early days of the park. Videos shown of that practice these days make bear experts cringe.

"A lot of people are very foolish in the way they interact with bears," Sailors said. "They actually feed the bears as if they're in a zoo and domesticated like pet dogs. They forget that these are wild creatures and occasionally you can come across one in a foul mood. It is plain stupid to feed wild animals like I have seen people do."

However, that was many years ago and in the interim human education about bears has been improved tremendously. There was a fall black bear hunting season in Wyoming when Sailors began his guide work, but usually his hunters shot bears less by design than as a byproduct of a hunt they were taking for another species.

"I never had a bear attack either myself or a hunter," Sailors said. "But I did have a hunter shoot one bear I didn't expect. I didn't want him shooting uphill at this black bear, but he did. When you hit a bear on a hill with a shot he'll roll right down the hill. They'll just curl up in a ball and come right down at you, if you're in the way. That's exactly what this old bear did. He rolled right past us. The bear rolled right past and he took another shot. Maybe because he knocked the leg out from under him, but the bear came down that hill in a hurry. You can never really predict bear behavior. You can only guess based on what's happened before. But typical is typical, only because sometimes a bear behaves atypically."

From the time their children were able to walk Kenny and Marilynne took Linda and Dan into the wilderness for trips. Sometimes they walked in the woods or the hills and other times they fished, sometimes for brook trout. They would camp overnight. One time they were fishing on a creek when Dan was perhaps four years old. Everyone was chatting and fishing and all of a sudden Linda yelled, "Where's Dan?"

"We were on a fast creek at flood stage in the spring," Sailors said. "We ran up and down that creek, Bokie and I, and we finally found the little tyke not far from the edge. He was standing there looking at the water. He had just gone for a walk. But it shows you how suddenly the wilderness can sneak up on you. It reminds you that there is potential danger everywhere. We flat tied him to a tree until we got camp made. Literally tied him up. We were pretty shook up."

Although Sailors majored in education at the University of Wyoming in order to become a teacher, before he even finished his classes he started thinking he'd rather work outdoors after he gave up basketball. His first idea was to become a forest ranger. That in itself was in lieu of becoming a cowboy since that job seemed in limited supply in the mid-twentieth century.

It should surprise no one that Sailors saw every cowboy movie he could when he was growing up and whenever he had the chance given his rural upbringing, whether it starred Tom Mix or Hopalong Cassidy or Roy Rogers. When they became available he read Louis L'Amour novels. The closest Sailors came to becoming a cowboy was during the summers in his high school years when he got the opportunity to work on a ranch. The idea of becoming a guide and outfitter superseded that.

Sailors learned how to shoot with a .22, but when he was in the Marines he learned about a .30.06.

"That's the first big gun I ever had," he said. "They trained us on that. Compared to a little old .22, that was a big difference, especially if you put it up against your shoulder. There was a good thump to it. The Marines taught me how to handle a pistol, too. All of the officers had .45s. You can see the common thread in all of these aspects of my growing up: Always around horses, always being in the outdoors, getting the chance to hunt early and learning more about guns in the military."

Although they had been married for a few years and had fished together and hiked together, Kenny and Bokie went on their first hunt together in 1946, on a morning trip out of Casper.

"It was pretty grassy, pretty green terrain," Sailors said, "and there was livestock in the general area, so you had to be careful. But the antelope were kind of down in little low spots between the swells. It was good terrain because you could stay out of sight. We spotted a big buck antelope and we spent some time stalking him. His horns were good-sized and he probably weighed close to two hundred pounds. I shot him with a Savage, a shot behind the front shoulder. Even with an antelope, which isn't as big as a moose, you've got six or eight inches you can shoot and get into his heart, lungs, or liver, the vital organs. He was a nice one and we had the head mounted and kept it for a long time."

The couple that hunts together stays together and Kenny and Bokie did stay together through all sorts of adventures.

In 1952, Kenny and Bokie started their boys ranch, essentially a summer camp, for boys nine to fifteen. He had just retired from playing basketball and in his first winter away from the game he traveled around the country promoting his new business to round up campers for five-week sessions.

"I talked with parents and teachers and showed movies of the area, just selling them on the idea that it was a good place to send boys for the summer," Sailors said. "The horseback riding was the thing. They loved that. Each kid had his own horse and he had to learn how to take care of it, to saddle it, to groom it, to feed it, the whole thing. We'd go back in the mountains near the Teton Wilderness area and we'd take the boys fishing, climbing mountains, and up on the snow. They swam. If some of the mothers had seen them after they'd been out in the hills for ten days they might not have appreciated it.

They were so dirty and grungy. They needed showers pretty badly. But it was a boy's fantasy. Usually, we went up the north fork of the Buffalo River and over the Continental Divide. We'd cross the Yellowstone River, too. Just the prettiest country you could find."

It worked out for a while, but Sailors said the weakest link in the operation was finding enough willing and responsible counselors who had the knowledge to operate in the wild. Sailors always accompanied the group—he led it— and he usually had a couple of cowboys along. The boys needed instruction and supervision. They came from all over the country, including New York, Minnesota, and Texas, and the program was also affiliated with the National Rifle Association so it included shooting lessons on a .22.

The defining moment when he decided to get out of the boys ranch business occurred one July when the group rode horses to Crater Lake. Sailors was called back to the ranch for some business and when he caught up to his people again he learned that those in charge in the interim had let the kids ride their horses onto some still-existing ice.

"On the ice with horses!" Sailors exclaimed. "I went home after that and said, 'Bokie, this is it. We're done with this.' I could see somebody getting killed and me being blamed for it."

After that they focused on the hunting trips.

Leading kids on a ride into the hills with the Grand Tetons in the background. (Photo courtesy Kenny Sailors.)

Once he was done with basketball, the boys camp was shut down, and fall hunting season ended, winter was pretty quiet for the Sailorses. But Sailors always watched wildlife in the winter when he could and in his neighborhood that meant moose as well as elk.

"Bokie and I used to play a game looking out the window of our ranch," Sailors said. "Moose would gather to browse among the willows out front near the river. With their dark brown color they'd blend right into the trees. We'd try to play a little game: How many moose were out there? Sometimes you really couldn't see a moose, but you knew they were out there. If you started studying you could see little tips of ears move here and there. It was almost like those Bev Doolittle paintings, the camouflage art, they call it. Maybe there would be fifteen moose out there in the trees, right up close.

"One thing basketball helped develop that continues to be an asset in spotting game is my peripheral vision. When you're hunting, especially in thick timber, that helps. You want to sense movement off to the sides, even if you're not facing it directly. Hunting a lot of times, all you'll get is a little clue, that tiny movement. After you see that, you try to focus on color or the shape of horns or legs. It's a lot knowing what to look for."

A major Wyoming hunting challenge was the pursuit of sheep. Sheep were not going to migrate past the front door. They were always at high elevations and seemingly unobtainable without putting some serious sweat into the effort. They were a prized species for energetic hunters, but often led the guide and his men on a merry chase. Sheep were difficult to corner, had excellent self-protective senses that made them difficult to reach for a good shot, and were fleet of foot. Any sheep hunt ran the risk of being confronted by bad weather in the high country. Snowfall was always a possibility.

As a horse lover, Sailors was always game to incorporate horses into his hunts. He and his clients rode to the hunting grounds and to a camp high up on mountains. The horses provided a head start, but they could not cope with the steepness of the terrain where the sheep hung out. The horses could help only so much. The rest of the hunt relied on the hunters' feet.

"Sheep are nearly always up high," Sailors said. "They're sure-footed and they spend their time on plateaus and narrow ridges, in nearly inaccessible country. You'd better be in good shape for sheep hunting. And they're different than most other animals in that often you can see them, but you can't get close enough to get a good shot."

Above all, that is the most significant challenge in bagging a sheep. If you can see the sheep, chances are the sheep can see you and if that happens the animal is gone in a flash.

"When you locate an animal, especially if he starts to move one way or the other, and you're in the thick trees where he can disappear behind brush, you really have to concentrate," Sailors said. "You have to anticipate. Where is he going to end up? Where's he going? Where's he headed for? That's like playing defense in basketball, actually. In basketball, you're looking for a good shot and you are in hunting, too. But the major difference is that in basketball you're in a hurry. In hunting you should be taking your time. That's a relative term, now that I think of it, because sometimes in hunting you've got to be in a hurry or you'll lose the shot for good. You have to shoot under control."

Some species are more difficult to track than others and sheep are right up there. In Wyoming that's a literal expression because sheep are mostly likely going to be found at elevations of around ten thousand feet. That's high where the air thins out and can affect breathing and thinking.

"There's no question that sheep hunting is the toughest of all big-game hunting," Sailors said. "Sheep are not going to come to you. You've got to go to them. And that means you've got to climb a mountain, sometimes two or three mountains. Sheep retreat to the very tops of mountains. Nonhunters don't really understand how much hunters prize sheep. Probably because the public at-large is fascinated by bears. They have this split view of bears as dangerous beasts, but also animals they see in the zoo that look harmless. Sheep are beautiful animals, though, and your thoughtful hunter would rather take a sheep than a bear. There are four kinds of sheep, the bighorn, desert ram, the stone, and Dall, or white, sheep. The horns and white cape are the attraction. They make a beautiful mount. But they are hard to get and there is quite a bit of status among sheep hunters to get them all."

Sheep meat, lamb, or mutton is a delicacy, and a horn with a measurement of thirty-six inches is a trophy. The largest sheep horn a Sailors client ever took was forty-three inches. Dall sheep can weigh three hundred pounds or more, so they grow quite large. A bighorn sheep, which has a tighter curl in the horn, can be a little bit bigger and the horns are larger.

Some animals move around over large acreage—that's common among bears. Some animals in different lands move around under cover of darkness and water at night. Sheep don't even bother with descending into valleys.

They need water, but usually find it at a much higher elevation than other animals do.

"Sheep often go up high and they often stay there," Sailors said. "They eat and drink on top of mountains. You wouldn't believe it. When you go up high into sheep country it's a regular sheep heaven up there. They have no need to come down. If they descend for water, it's only to a lesser altitude, but usually there's water up near the top. They can get real cozy up high. For one thing they don't like mosquitoes and bugs and they can avoid them at high altitude. They have excellent eyes and can see for great distances. The higher up they are, the more they can see."

One of the most important tools of the trade for sheep hunters is binoculars. Oftentimes that is the only way sheep are spotted except from great distances when their bodies may simply be white dots against the landscape. When Sailors was a novice guide he didn't always quiz his clients on their conditioning in advance when they were booking sheep hunts. He learned quickly, though, that he had to know what they could do.

An early client did not discuss a problem he had in the mountains until he was in the mountains: He was scared of heights.

"That's kind of a liability when you're walking along mountain ridges," Sailors said. "I asked him, 'Why on earth would you go sheep hunting then?' He said, 'I didn't realize it would be like that.'"

That's like taking a cruise to the Antarctic when you get seasick. Sailors began to worry that his hunter wasn't going to make it through the trip and that he would have to pack him off the mountain instead of packing a sheep off. That taught him a lesson, so that early in correspondence with a potential client he began to ask if he was in top shape and if he was scared of heights since they would not be taking an elevator to the top of any mountains.

"Sheep hunting is no picnic, especially if you want to get a trophy sheep," Sailors said. "You're going to have to work for it. You might have to climb a mountain every day for six or seven days to get in position to get a good shot. Maybe every day for the whole hunt. I suppose that scares some people off. A typical sheep hunt takes a lot of effort. They're elusive and you don't find them on every mountain and you don't find them every time you go out. Bighorn sheep are a lot tougher to spot than the white, Dall sheep. Bighorn sheep are a lot darker. They look like the mountain. They're a stone color, grayish, darkish, though they do have a white rump. If they're bedded down, of course, you don't

Kenny Sailors (right) led his hunters on pursuit of sheep in the mountains of Wyoming and Alaska and the trips involved visiting high country in remote areas. (Photo courtesy Kenny Sailors.)

see the white rump. I've glassed a mountain for several hours and not seen a thing. Then, all of a sudden, at the right time of day, they begin to get up and move around. You see the white rumps and the movement and you realize they were there all along."

Patience, patience, patience is the main rule in sheep hunting and stamina, stamina, stamina is probably rule number two. Another element that works against hunters is the wind. If they are downwind of the sheep their stalk is doomed. With the wind blowing the wrong way a hunter doesn't have a chance against what will soon be a skittish sheep poised to bolt if it sniffs the wrong smell. Even the wind's cooperation doesn't guarantee success.

"You don't walk right up to a sheep even if the wind conditions are right," Sailors said. "Even if the wind is blowing your scent the other way. They're always up above you, looking down on you and they've got the best eyes of any animal there is probably. So they see you long before you see them. Your best bet is to come on them from the top of the mountain. I tried to get a hunter out of camp and up in the mountains before the sheep bed down. The hotter it is the earlier they'll get ready for a nap. For sure, if you don't get up there before noon you're guaranteed to miss them. They feed first thing in the morning, get their bellies full, then they lay down to rest and watch for enemies."

Sometimes when Sailors guided a hunter for sheep he didn't even carry his own rifle. He knew he was not going to hunt. His job was to lead the client to the animal. However, once in the Wyoming high country his hunter gut-shot a ram and only wounded it. Sailors recognized that it wasn't going to die easily. It began weaving in and out of some rocks and started climbing higher on the mountain. In the sheep's mind going up equated moving to safety. The hunter, though, was out of gas. He couldn't go on. In good conscience, Sailors could not leave the animal.

"We were falling behind," he said. "I was making a lot better time than the hunter was. So was the bighorn, though. Finally, I could see it was going to get away from us. I borrowed the hunter's gun to take the shot. I shot uphill and I got him. It was an even tougher shot because it was with a gun that I wasn't used to. He did have a good scope on it. I shot that sheep at between 350 and 400 yards. To tell you the truth, it was pretty much luck. I didn't kill him with the first shot and I had to shoot him a second time. It was probably the toughest long shot I've made."

As the guide Sailors felt a responsibility to the sheep to put it out of its misery and to the client so he could get the horns from the sheep he shot. If he didn't take the shot at the moment he chose to, the sheep was going to disappear over the hill and leave the humans in its dust.

When Sailors watches western movies or other action films and the hero makes a long distance shot he often scoffs. He knows what they're doing is virtually impossible. He laughs even harder if the police officer or private detective or spy fires off his guns and hits the bad guy while he is on the run. Shooting on the run while hunting is a no-no and the likelihood of hitting anything while the legs are churning is slim.

CHAPTER 13

Cowboying Up
and on to Alaska

FROM THE TIME HE WAS A BOY, Kenny Sailors loved to ride horses. Since he wasn't going to be riding on cattle roundups on the old Chisholm Trail or anything approximating it, he felt fortunate to be able to incorporate horseback riding into his hunts.

"The first horse I ever had was named Paint," Sailors said. "Sounds like the name of a horse John Wayne rode in one of his movies, doesn't it? But that was before John Wayne was making those cowboy pictures that made him famous. My mother was born in Kansas in 1881 and she was fifteen when her family moved west to Colorado. They went by covered wagon. My mother grew up in a sod house with a dirt floor. They had the occasional rattlesnake come to visit, too. It was a real western life. I have always been interested in the old West, in preserving that style of life and my wife, Bokie, and I lived our lives pretty close to the way we might have if we'd been born many years earlier."

Sailors never did go after bad guys or anything like that, but his hunting guide business was his way of staying in touch with the wilderness and the West. He also simply enjoyed being outdoors, inhaling nature. There was plenty of outdoors to go around in Wyoming.

"More than anything, I suppose, being outdoors was special to me," he said. "I think you get that in your blood when you're young and it never goes away. Watching the animals, I liked lying around just watching the clouds, watching the birds. I studied them, the way they fly. Anything about nature. Big stuff, little stuff, any of it, I liked. I've watched anthills by the hour. I just watched how a bunch of ants worked together. It's fascinating. It is hard for me

The old cowboy, as Kenny Sailors considered himself, in Western dress in Gakona, Alaska, in the 1990s. (Photo by Lew Freedman.)

to understand how a person can deny the existence of God when they observe nature and His handiwork."

Horses were integral to the Sailors guiding business. He wore a cowboy hat when he rode into the mountains. His signature white hat was so creased and stained and bent that it looked older than the hills. He also had hand-me-down spurs and chaps that were even older. People gazed at their worn look and asked Sailors if they predated the settling of the West.

"I've had that stuff a long time," Sailors said, referring to spurs that would now be more than ninety years old. "People wondered why I wore chaps, but when you got into the snow and sleet and rain they came in handy."

Sailors was most at home in the wild and he was an observant traveler, taking note of twists and turns in the terrain, of small markings that could help lead him and his hunters back to camp or back home. He was always paying attention, making sure he had the way back mapped out in his mind.

He became expert at reading signs like that and his ability to absorb that information frustrated his wife because when he was driving around cities he was always getting lost or making wrong turns.

"Why don't you do that in town?" Bokie said to him. "You can't find anything in town."

Perhaps because finding one's way down from high elevation and sometimes in the snow could be a matter of life and death.

Sailors built his business over time at the Heart 6 Ranch, specializing in those hard-core mountain hunting trips for bears, sheep, elk, and moose. Usually, things went smoothly and the hunter got what he was after. Other times hunts were memorable for things going wrong or spectacularly right. When something unusual happened in the field it stuck out and stuck in memory. Sailors needed helpers in his business, or assistant guides, but discovered that reliable and top-notch assistants were at a premium. In Sailors's mind a hunt was the composite of many parts. It meant camping in the wild, hiking in the wild, climbing mountains, riding horses, stalking animals, taking good shots, and then hauling meat and trophy antlers home. He very much wanted the trip to be a good time for all and not simply an efficient shoot.

"A hunt should be a total experience," Sailors said. "There are a few guides that never learn this, I'm afraid. Their whole attitude on life is different. They shouldn't even be in the guiding business, some of them, but they are. They've got the title and they've got the license. I've had assistant guides in my time who were in excellent physical condition. They could shoot. They were good hunters. But when it came to their personality and getting along with the hunter, being patient with him, recognizing that he's a little on the old side, that he shouldn't be forced to go too fast, or that he has some kind of handicap, they were practically worthless because they couldn't adjust. You get young guides, in particular, it seems, who just want to show the hunter how macho they are."

After his first few years in business guiding in Wyoming Sailors didn't even have to advertise. All of his clients were either repeat customers or friends of previous customers who had heard good things about him. Sailors took that pattern to mean that his hunters had had a good time.

Although horses have always been part of his hunts, they are not used in hunting in most parts of the United States or the world. Much depends on terrain, horse availability, and the best way to reach the hunting grounds. For Sailors using horses has been a perk because he loved riding so much. His animals were workhorses, part of the crew, hauling supplies and gear, as well as hunters. They were not thoroughbred athletes of the type that compete in the Kentucky Derby, or Budweiser Clydesdales.

"Most people don't associate horses with hunting," Sailors said. "In this type of business, you look for a horse that's gentle, one that's still got some spirit and will go without you having to kick him, but at the same time gentle enough that he's not dangerous for a hunter to ride. You don't want a horse that kicks or bites, or has a mean streak. You want a horse that's sound. You want a big horse, not a horse that's just a pony."

Ideally a Sailors horse weighed a thousand to thirteen hundred pounds and was sturdy. He wanted strong horses that were relaxed enough to carry a big man across a flowing stream without panic. Good-sized horses with broader backs were able to haul more meat out of camp from a hunt, too, as much as half of a moose on one horse.

"When I first started guiding, I knew how to ride, but I wasn't much of an expert on packing," Sailors said. "It's quite an art, packing a horse. You have a tendency to overload. I can testify to that. But if you don't balance the load just right the ropes get loose and the pack will shift. It starts swaying from side to side and pretty soon it turns under the horse. You might injure the horse or lose some essential equipment, or at the least you're going to have a big mess

Kenny loved guiding by horseback. The photo was taken in Wyoming in October 1960. (Photo courtesy Kenny Sailors.)

to clean up. And not always in a convenient spot. It's not easy to repack a horse on a narrow trail on a ridge. It can also be dangerous for you and the horse."

Horses are actually smart enough to know when the packing job is a poor one and they resist heading off down the trail and can be as stubborn as mules that have that reputation. It was important to Sailors's operation to have reliable packhorses because the terrain he hunted was so rugged it was impossible to land an airplane. The ride in also took ten hours in the saddle at a rate of about a mile an hour from home. He needed trustworthy horses.

The first time that Sailors used horses for packing gear into the wild he made a deal to buy some horses from a friend who dabbled in rodeo stock. While Sailors had a sufficient supply of riding animals he needed work animals. The friend said he would come along on the first trip to make sure everything worked out well.

Things went wrong from the start. When it was departure time only one horse was packed. Sailors and his friend had to blindfold most of the horses to keep them calm enough to be loaded. Turns out the friend was providing horses that were bucking broncos in the rodeo. They were led into camp, unloaded, and a hired hand started to bring them back home with the empty boxes strapped on. Partway back one horse banged into a tree, became agitated, and set off a crazed stampede in the string. The horses went wild and threw off the gear as they ran loose through the countryside, littering the ground with Heart 6 Ranch equipment. One box didn't turn up until years later. It took a few adjustment trips for those rough-riding broncs to tame down enough to ride as pack animals.

Over time Sailors had three hunting camps that became headquarters at different times in the search for elk. They were at the Yellowstone River, the Soda Fork of the Buffalo River, and Two Ocean Pass. They were situated at between 7,000 and 8,000 feet of elevation. Sometimes he led horses over a 12,800-foot pass. Typically, Sailors had a maximum of four hunters in camp at once. Any more seemed to be a crowd. The busiest season he had called for seventy horses and mules running back and forth to the camps, thirty-five of them leased.

One of Sailors's regulars was a man named Tommy Morrison who began hunting with him in Wyoming in 1952 and hunted every year with the operation through 1964. Most hunts were ten days to two weeks long, but one year Morrison came and hung out for the entire couple-month season in the Jackson Hole area. It turned into a solid investment of time because Sailors forevermore referred to Morrison's visit as "the perfect hunt."

"I define a good hunt as one where your hunters get all the game they came for," Sailors said. "They all have decent heads and maybe one, or even two, in the bunch get a real trophy. One might even make the record book. I never had another situation in Wyoming where one hunter got everything. I've got a picture of me with Tommy's moose, bear, elk, and mule deer. If he had drawn a permit he could even have got a nice ram. We ran into one and took some pictures. That hunt was like sweeping the World Series."

Friend Tommy had been an industrious, hardworking furniture company owner in Houston who worked so hard he gave himself a stroke at thirty-two. Doctors and friends recommended regular getaways and spending time each fall at the Heart 6 Ranch on hunting trips filled the bill.

"We were his haven in the wilderness and each season he'd go out hunting with us," Sailors said.

Gradually, Tommy made the ranch his home away from home, coming to visit before hunting season, bringing hard-to-get fresh vegetables, and eventually becoming as good in the wilderness as Sailors's assistant guides. Sailors even bought some of his ranch furniture through Tommy. Each season Tommy also lost weight, considerable weight, though he did usually put it back on over the rest of the year.

"He knew it all," Sailors said of Tommy's growing expertise. "He could pack, he could ride, he could hunt, camp out, help other hunters zero their rifles in. Tommy was an excellent shot himself. He was a real good hunter and he loved it all."

The last animal Tommy, who spent much of his hunt time with assistant guide Jim Williams while Sailors saw to the needs of other clients, harvested in his special season was an elk.

"I don't recall another hunter ever getting all those big-game animals in one season," Sailors said. "It may have been done, but not with me, and I don't remember hearing about it."

One of Sailors's other regulars, Zach Taylor from Michigan, played an unwitting role in his favorite guide getting revenge on a competing guide who was breaking the rules of the area. Each registered guide had an assigned territory, but Sailors discovered through some errant tracks leading him to a makeshift empty camp that another guide was poaching on his territory.

Without telling Taylor, he enlisted him in his plan to rid himself of the problem. On the first day of the hunt Sailors led Taylor into the area where the stranger had scouted elk and was trying to set it up for one of his own hunters, Sailors figured. Sailors set Taylor up about three-quarters of a mile from the intruder's camp where a large bull roamed.

"The way we were hunting elk was by the use of a whistle," Sailors said. "We would blow this whistle and it made an elk sound. It sounds shrill, high-pitched. You can really attract elk that way. They hear it and then an older bull will come toward you thinking you're another bull with cows. This whistle is fight talk."

Sailors and Taylor hiked to a higher elevation, working up a sweat, and then heard an elk whistle. Sailors recognized it as an artificial sound, another whistle, and guessed that the rogue guide was trying to lure a bull elk down the mountain. About ten seconds later they heard an elk bugle from a ridge above and Sailors told Taylor they were going after that animal. The other guide and his hunter whistled every few minutes. Sailors and Taylor were positioned between the bull on the ridge and other men.

"Pretty soon the whistling sound of the one from the top got closer," Sailors said, "and closer still." It was the real bull. "Zach and I worked our way through the brush, side-hilling across these rides and draws. The elk would walk down the ridge, kind of staying in the cover of the trees. He did a good job of staying out of sight. He was working his way down."

Quietly, Sailors and Taylor kept up their stalk, crossing ridges, closing the distance. They got close enough to see the bull stretch his neck and bugle, a fascinating nature sight. It was a six-point bull and when Taylor had an opening in the trees he fired the fatal shot. The bull went down hit. The other guide immediately recognized the significance and pulled out, never to interfere with Sailors's hunting grounds again. Sailors never even told Taylor what was going on as the backdrop of his hunt.

Sheep hunting wasn't for everyone, but in Wyoming, elk hunting seemed to be for everyone who lived there. It was the game meat of choice and most of the hunters were after elk to fill their freezer with meat that could be parceled out at the dinner table over the next year.

"More people hunt elk in Wyoming than anything else," Sailors said. "It's the meat animal for the resident hunter. Elk aren't as big as Alaska moose, but a big bull elk will go eight hundred pounds. That's a big animal no matter how you look at it."

During his nineteen years hunting in Wyoming Sailors was sometimes surprised by elk behavior. Typically, the sheep are the animals that climb high and elk don't even think of going near the top of mountains. They prefer to stay shadowy in the trees a bit lower. On one hunt Sailors was near the top of a peak and heard the clatter of rocks. That was a sheep indicator.

"All of a sudden we heard this snorting and breathing and turned around and there were three big bull elk," he said. "One of them was a royal, a very large bull. They'd come all the way up from the Thoroughfare Drainage. They'd moved up into sheep country. Their tongues were still hanging out from the climb. The only time elk go up high as a rule is during rutting season. They can be really hard to hunt when they do that. They're easier to hunt when you can bugle for them. They're thinking of other things, you know. They've got cows with them and their minds aren't quite as sharp."

The time Sailors bumped into the three bulls high up on the mountain he wasn't on an elk hunt. He hadn't even brought a camera, so his only image of the huffing and puffing animals is in his memory.

Once, one of Sailors's friends named Mendel Collins was on a hunt, but his goal was just to shoot a spike, a smaller elk, for winter meat. Collins was a Nazarene minister and he was popular in the hunting camp because he always chipped in with the chores, chopping wood, cooking, and taking care of the horses. On this occasion as the hunt was winding down the men hadn't seen any prospects and were running out of time. Then in midmorning a small herd of elk was spotted through binoculars. The elk were fairly distant and they were on the move, away from Sailors and Collins. Sailors did not think it was possible to sneak up on them without being seen and expressed his skepticism to Collins over the poor likelihood of success. He suggested an unusual plan, which was to stay on the horses for a while and try to close the distance to the elk rather than a stealth approach on foot.

"We could even see the route they would follow to escape from us," Sailors said. "There was a trail right over the top of the mountain. We decided to give it a try, though. We rode towards them and they hadn't all sensed us yet. We climbed off the horses and tied them up and we crouched over and started moving up on them. As we got closer several elk saw us."

Well, that was that, Sailors was sure. One by one the elk rose to their feet and started ambling over the top of the mountain. The elk were too far away to allow for a good shot. Sailors and Collins kept moving ahead and all of the elk cleared out but one. It turned out to be a spike, just what Collins was after.

"That crazy animal started out to go over the hill, just like the others had,"

Sailors said. "But then he stopped to look back at us. He looked down at us and then he looked off the other way where the other elk had gone. He did that a couple of times, as if he was trying to decide what to do. It was obvious that the natural thing for him to do was to join the other elk. But for some reason, he didn't. He started coming down a little ways, towards us. He'd hesitate and stand there. Look back and then come a little more towards us."

Sailors could not figure out why the elk was behaving in this manner. It made no sense at all. Sailors glanced over at Collins and then did a double take. The minister was praying.

"Now, I'm a great believer in prayer," Sailors said, "I don't mind telling you, but I didn't expect this. Mendel kept praying and that elk kept coming."

When the elk got within a hundred yards of the men, Collins stopped praying, picked up his rifle, and shot the elk. He had his store of meat for the year.

"Kenny," Collins said, "that's exactly what I've been praying for ever since we left camp this morning. Praise the Lord!"

In the Midwestern states densely populated with deer, vehicle-deer accidents are common. They are counted in the thousands each year and insurance companies put out statistics about their frequency as part of their warnings to motorists to drive safely. In Alaska, the worst scenario is for cars to collide with moose, which are much bigger than deer and can cause much more damage to an automobile. The same driving principles and threat held true in Wyoming. In the Jackson Hole area the Sailorses were always conscious of the possibility of smacking into a moose, deer, or an elk.

One day Bokie almost had a triple-header, clipping one of each kind. She was on her way to pick up daughter Linda at some event and was driving very slowly because she definitely feared the possibility of creaming an animal. On the way back to the Heart 6 Ranch, just outside of Jackson Hole, a group of mule deer appeared and she had to swerve to miss them. Driving another twenty miles Bokie came to a place on the road where many accidents had occurred between cars and moose. Her own kids were getting to be of driver's age and she always admonished them to "Slow down, even if you don't see one." A cow moose appeared out of nowhere and she hit the animal.

"It was too late to stop," Sailors said. "She scooped her right up and her back was flat against the windshield, all four legs hanging down in front of the hood. The moose was kicking and squirming until she kicked herself right off the car and ran off."

It was a low-impact crash because of the slow speed, so Bokie resumed driving home. She drove roughly another half mile and nearly slammed into a bull elk.

"The road was like an obstacle course that day," Sailors said. "It was the spring and things were starting to move around. She was hyper. [And had quite a story to tell.] It took us a while to calm down."

By 1965, the Sailorses had been married for more than two decades. Daughter Linda was grown and son Dan had just completed high school. They had been lifelong residents of Wyoming, except for Kenny's connection to various cities when he played basketball, and were well entrenched in their guiding business. They just weren't sure they wanted to continue doing the same thing in the same place forever.

From the time he captained the University of Wyoming basketball team to the NCAA title, was hailed as an All-American basketball player, and was selected as college basketball's player of the year in 1943, the name Sailors was well-known to most residents of the state. Between 1954 and 1956, soon after retiring from professional basketball, Sailors had served a term in the Wyoming state legislature. He also ran for the US House of Representatives twice in the 1950s without success.

Conservative by nature, concerned about the political state of the country, as well as conservation issues, in 1964 Sailors decided to reenter politics. He ran in the Republican primary for the US Senate, but lost and then became state chairman for Arizona Republican Barry Goldwater's presidential race.

This was basically a year after the assassination of the popular Democratic President John F. Kennedy and his successor, former vice president Lyndon Baines Johnson, had assumed the office. LBJ began moving the country toward a "Great Society" with his domestic programs, and although he did not realize it yet was presiding over the country being sucked into one of its most divisive conflicts in South Vietnam. The war in Southeast Asia would become his undoing by 1968 when he chose not to run for reelection. However, in 1964 Goldwater was viewed by many voters as an extremist with warlike tendencies. When the vote was counted, the Democrats had won a landslide and LBJ's coattails had been very strong, dragging his party's congressmen to victory all over the nation. In a sense, politically, Sailors went down with Goldwater. He seemed to have explored all of his statewide political options and although he had name recognition he did not win a major elective office.

At the time, Sailors was also concerned by what he considered to be a growing trend toward excessive regulation of hunting laws, the outdoors, and other state rules that could limit the way he did business as a guide.

"Government regulation was starting to interfere with everything," was Sailors's opinion. "Wyoming was starting to go to permits. They were placing limits on how many animals could be hunted and it was getting tougher for commercial hunting. I understand when a species gets down in numbers you have to have constraints. There can be overkilling and sometimes disease will reduce the size of a herd of elk. Plus, other things happen that you haven't counted on like heavy snow years that cause starvation.

"But you need smart game management, too. You have to anticipate things. If an area is overhunted close the area down for two, three, or five years, don't regulate the whole state. Shut down that region. Manage the area. That's what the state officials are supposed to be doing, isn't it?"

Loss of the election and the changing manner in which the outdoors was being regulated combined to frustrate Sailors. He and Bokie liked rural areas and the Jackson Hole area was growing fast. He felt all of Wyoming's cities might be growing too large for his taste.

"Bokie and I probably liked people more than the average person does, but we just didn't like them climbing over us and looking in our back window," Sailors said.

Before Kenny and Bokie even got married they talked about Alaska as a fantasy-type place. To them in the 1940s it seemed just like Wyoming, only more so. They had never visited The Last Frontier, as Alaska was called, but by 1965 when they first seriously entertained the notion of moving north, it had become a state. Another major reason why the lifelong Wyoming residents thought of moving to Alaska was the deterioration in Bokie's breathing. Doctors told them she would be much better off if they moved to a place that wasn't as high as Wyoming's elevation, specifically under three thousand feet where the air would be thicker. And Alaska seemed to have everything Wyoming did except for their friends.

"It was the wildness, the bigness of it, that we liked," Sailors said. "It was the same as Wyoming used to be, only more. It was bigger. There was more big game. There's more of everything. Wyoming is beautiful, beautiful country. We had a lot of friends and relatives there. But Alaska had a special appeal for us. We got to talking about moving to Alaska and becoming hunting guides there after the elections in the fall of 1964. The thing that dawned on me very early in my political career, though, was that you couldn't be an idealist. You might have some ideas, but you have anywhere from 50 to 150 legislators to convince that you're right."

In 1964 Sailors was running on a platform that pretty much was built around keeping Wyoming the same way it had been.

"Being a ranch boy who was raised out-of-doors, I was a strong believer in individualism," Sailors said. "I wanted to see that strain stay in Wyoming. I didn't like a lot of the change I was seeing. I wanted to preserve all of the good things about Wyoming that I liked and that made it possible to make a good living in the outdoors. I never really thought I was going to win in 1964. In fact, Bokie and I were planning the move to Alaska even before the election results were in. The other times I really thought I was going to win. It was close, but I didn't. And, of course, I lost and we moved to Alaska. The prospect of being a hunting guide in Alaska was exciting. If the Super Bowl is the ultimate football game, then Alaska is the ultimate for a hunter. It seemed like the place to be. We also wanted to homestead and you could still get land in Alaska."

Ever since the Alaska Gold Rush, the lure of the Far North had dazzled residents of the lower forty-eight states and convinced them it was a special place to start their lives fresh. Go north, young men, was the theme. Start over. Alaska is far more sophisticated and grown up now than it was in 1898, just after World War II, or in 1965 when Kenny and Bokie Sailors aimed their automobile at the forty-ninth state.

It is still referred to as The Last Frontier, and despite the modernization of Alaska, it is still as wild a place that remains on earth. Sailors was right to think it bore a strong resemblance to Wyoming, yet offered the same outdoor treats over a broader swath of land.

With daughter Linda grown and married, and son Dan a recent high school graduate, their parents were free enough to drive north, to point their vehicle vaguely toward Anchorage or Fairbanks by traversing the bumpy, dirt road of the Alaska Highway.

They didn't know where they were going for sure, but Alaska promised fresh adventure, more wild country, and a hunting paradise. For the Sailorses, at that point in their lives, that was all they needed to know.

CHAPTER 14

Alaska Life

ONCE HE GOT OUT OF THE BASKETBALL BUSINESS Kenny Sailors lived with a simple philosophy in Wyoming. He felt, "I always had my hunting to fall back on to make a living." Well, he had the same idea in mind when he and his Mrs. set out from Wyoming for Alaska by driving the Alaska Highway that had been built during World War II to facilitate the movement of troops and supplies north.

When the Sailorses thought of the outdoors, it was always accompanied by fresh air. The purer the air, the better off Bokie was because she had to cope with her emphysema. The Alaska Highway was not was paved at the time, and it took decades before it was mostly turned into asphalt. The road was rutted, and could be hard on tires and windshields as pebbles were churned up and tossed off the glass. If there was no rain the highway was also very dusty.

Other than Alaska in general, the Sailorses did not have a destination picked out to settle. Of course they had heard of the bigger cities of Anchorage and Fairbanks, but just as they were not likely to base their operations in Cheyenne or Laramie because those were cities, they weren't particularly likely to set up a new home in Alaska's largest cities.

As they drove the fourteen hundred miles of the Alaska Highway, the dirt and dust began to bother Bokie more and more. The Sailorses had passed through Whitehorse in the Yukon Territory and crossed the Alaska border. They turned off the Alaska Highway onto the Richardson Highway that connected Fairbanks to Valdez, but was basically a very rural area. There were few restaurants or hotels or other signs of development on their route. Not that they minded that. It was exactly the type of country they appreciated.

But Bokie started to feel ill and the dust was gathering in her throat and causing her serious shortness of breath.

"She needed doctors," Sailors said. "She needed a hospital. The way we came the only hospital between Whitehorse and Anchorage was in Glennallen. That dust was just killing her. You couldn't get away from it. It's everywhere. We were forced to stop. The dust was so terrible that we had to stop to get help for her. She said, 'Kenny, I just can't go anymore.'"

They had passed through the Yukon, to Tok, and were planning to head to Valdez, where the terminus of the Trans-Alaska Pipeline System was later constructed. Glennallen is a small town that is located about two hundred miles from Anchorage (even today it has fewer than five hundred people) where the Richardson and Glenn Highways intersect. The coincidence of Bokie's need, medical treatment availability, and friendly local folks combined to prevent the Sailorses from driving on.

"We didn't necessarily pick out Glennallen as a place for us to stop and spend thirty-five years, but the reason we stopped was for her health," Sailors said. "We tried to leave there a time or two, but every time we tried to get away from there toward Valdez or up to Fairbanks or Anchorage, why she'd get to breathing bad again. And that was the only hospital."

Glennallen was the largest town in the vicinity, but the Sailorses actually stopped in Gakona, first, about fifteen miles shy of the intersection of the roads, where a family named McMahan (about to become their best friends in Alaska) operated a trailer park.

After obtaining medicine for Bokie they thought they would hang around for a couple of days before returning to the road. The first time they attempted to drive toward Valdez, "we didn't get very far before she didn't feel well again. We pulled off into a camping area."

The next time they attempted an escape the Sailorses drove about ten miles toward Anchorage before Bokie felt sick again. They turned around and drove back to Gakona.

"Little did we know when we stopped that time we were stopping for good," Sailors said.

The Sailorses arrived in Alaska on July 4, 1965. They knew there was going to be a waiting period to establish residency as a local guide, so the very first thing Kenny did was buy a dated fishing license as proof of his residence. One of the first things Sailors discovered was that Alaska had just about as many hunting regulations as Wyoming, it seemed. He could not walk right in and start a guide operation.

"The rule they had was that you had to be an assistant guide to a registered guide for three years and you had to take a minimum of two hunters out in each of those years," Sailors said. "Then you had to get recommendations from the hunters. At the end of the three-year period you could take a written test. And if you passed that with a good score you were able to take an oral test. Obviously, they were making it tough to become a guide."

Just about five minutes after showing up in the neighborhood Sailors looked up an old guide friend in the area that he knew from Wyoming named Don DeHart and informed him of his ambitions. The funny part was that the Sailorses, being new to Alaska and with a certain lack of familiarity with the midnight sun, dropped in on DeHart at three-thirty in the morning. They had been fooled by the long hours of daylight in Alaska in early July.

"He thought we were crazy," Sailors said.

After the oops moment, though, his contact set Sailors on the road to fulfilling the assistant guide requirements. Meanwhile, son Dan, who had planned to remain in Wyoming, decided with a friend that Alaska sounded like a great place for them, too. While he had made the call to stay behind, now he wanted to join his parents in the north.

He was in Cheyenne when he made the choice a few months after they left and in November of the same year he also became an Alaskan.

"I wanted to come, too," said Dan Sailors, who currently lives in Aniak, Alaska, a small village west of Anchorage off the Alaska road system. "I was done with high school and drove with a friend."

Unlike his father, whom he calls "Pop," the younger Sailors was not an accomplished basketball player.

"I tried," he said, "but I wasn't very good. Skiing was my forte and then I broke my leg. That put the kibosh on that."

Kenny knew that it was going to take some time to become a full-time guide and that he needed another profession to make a living. For the first time since graduating, Sailors put his education degree from Wyoming to use and became a high school teacher and basketball coach.

For starters, Kenny and Bokie became close friends with the McMahan family and they moved into the trailer court. The father was named Cleo and the mother was named Daphne and there were two boys and a girl in the clan.

Later, the two boys, Chuck and Harley, worked as guides for what became a shared Sailors-McMahan guide service, as did Dan Sailors when he got a bit older. After their aborted efforts to depart the area for Anchorage, Valdez, or Fairbanks, Kenny and Bokie stuck with the trailer court in Gakona, on the outskirts of Glennallen.

"We ended up deciding, 'What the heck, let's just stay here,'" Sailors said. "The trailer park wasn't fancy. They had water and sewage."

Knowing that Kenny was looking for a teaching job, Daphne McMahan, who knew the superintendent of schools, put in a good word for him.

"She talked to the superintendent, who was actually the principal at Glennallen High School, too, since they didn't have much money," Sailors said. "She might have been on the school board at the time, too."

Bokie and Daphne quickly became friendly and it was Bokie who told Daphne about Kenny's background as a basketball star and a former professional.

"She was kind of taken in by that," Sailors said. "We were living in her trailer court with our little Air Stream trailer." Apparently Sailors's credentials translated well and the superintendent took a road trip to Gakona to see Kenny. "He told me what the deal was. He said, 'We can't pay you much because we don't have any money. That's why we're so short on people. We don't even have girls' basketball in the school, volleyball, or anything. We can't afford it.'"

Title IX, the federal legislation that became the great equalizer in terms of opportunity was not approved by Congress until 1973, so numerous schools around the country did not have much in the way of interscholastic sports offerings for girls.

Glennallen was actually ahead of the times by even considering the addition of such teams. Up until the 1970s girls' basketball was pretty much an afterthought at most institutions, but was also played in a different manner. During the dark ages of girls' high school sports when schools even started girls' basketball teams the players were restricted to an oddball kind of game with six players, not five, to a side, and with some prevented from crossing half-court. Not only was it thought to be unladylike to sweat, but girls were not given credit for having much stamina and it was felt they couldn't run up and down the court like the boys.

There were hardly any girls' basketball teams in Alaska, though a few private religious schools, such as Monroe Catholic in Fairbanks, fielded teams. A few other small schools in the Glennallen region had some girls' teams, too. One private school took in Alaska Native Eskimos and Indians at a boarding school because their villages did not have high schools. Not until the dispersal of oil money in the next decade once the Alaska Pipeline was up and operating and victory in a lawsuit did Alaska's legislature appropriate money to fund the construction of high schools in villages in remote areas of the state. Prior to that development Natives were forced to leave home to gain a high school diploma.

After the superintendent told Sailors that he had no money to start any girls' program and could only pay him for teaching, Kenny said that he thought there should be sports for girls.

"I really want athletics for my girls," Sailors said. "It's just as good for them as it is for the boys. The superintendent said, 'We couldn't pay you anything.' I said, 'I don't need to be paid, and I don't even know if I'm going to stay in Glennallen, but if I take the job, I'll consider giving you a hand anyway in coaching some girls in the Glennallen area.'"

Also located in the area was a religious group called the Central Alaskan Mission, which was of Baptist faith, and that organization also ran a school in the area. There was basketball interest there, as well.

Living in the trailer park was always meant to be temporary, but the Sailorses really didn't know where they wanted to settle before starting a guide service. Cleo McMahan played a role in the fact that Kenny and Bokie stayed in Gakona. Once they decided to explore the area McMahan said he knew of a spot that was just perfect for a homestead. It was a place he and his wife had scouted, but they already had a homestead. It was right along the Richardson Highway in Gakona, convenient to Glennallen and not far from the trailer park.

"Kenny, I know where there's a beautiful spot," McMahan told Sailors. McMahan was a good salesman, though it didn't take much convincing once he described the assets of the adjacent Gulkana River. "That river has three kinds of salmon and it has rainbow trout and Dolly Varden and grayling. You can kill your moose meat right on the river if you want to, and caribou, they're right in this area."

The Sailorses loved it. "That's where we built our lodge," Sailors said. The lodge was on a hill and beneath it flowed the river. "We decided to homestead there."

While getting used to living in Alaska, the first thing Sailors did was help organize the Glennallen girls' basketball team. The first team had almost nobody to play against except for the several private religious schools.

"The other schools didn't have girls' athletics," Sailors said. "No money.

Kenny Sailors and wife, Marilynne (Bokie), at their cabin in Gakona, Alaska. Bokie died in 2002 after the couple's fifty-nine years of marriage. (Photo by Lew Freedman.)

Then the [Glennallen] boys' coach left, so they didn't have a coach for that team either. I said I would handle both of them, that I'd just coach both. For several years, up until about 1973, I coached the boys' varsity, the boys' junior varsity, and the girls' varsity. The girls' didn't have a junior varsity. It was pretty tough. I was a busy man, but I enjoyed it."

The first year, when Sailors accompanied the boys' team to the state tournament in Fairbanks he went around to the cheerleaders for other schools and tried to convince them to help get girls' teams started at their schools.

"We ended up with nine or ten teams that were actually playing," he said. "Anchorage hadn't come in yet. Then the University of Alaska got interested in Fairbanks. I scolded them for not having girls' athletics in college or high school. They didn't even have a university in Anchorage yet. I went to Fairbanks and they told me 'Kenny, we don't have the money in this state. There's not enough people. There's no tax base. All the money we get is from the state or from donations."

Even the teams playing operated on a shoestring with inferior equipment to the boys. That was one of the items addressed by Title IX when it passed and changed the landscape across the country for girls' sports.

"What we got was rubber balls for basketballs," Sailors said of his early years coaching the Glennallen girls' team. "I hadn't been around girls players before, but I knew a little bit about basketball. The first thing I told the superintendent was, 'If you want to keep me here as a coach we're getting rid of that girls' game nonsense, the half-court game,' and he agreed with me. We started out playing the half-court, but the teams we were playing agreed to the change, too. We changed over before the end of the first season."

During Sailors's first season in charge of the Glennallen team the University of Alaska in Fairbanks invited the girls' teams to play a tournament at the end of the year and Glennallen won it.

"The next year we had more teams, probably about fifteen, and I was getting them mostly through those cheerleaders," Sailors said. "I would just tell them, 'If you want to play basketball, just lobby your school to start a team. You can always find somebody to coach you. Don't worry about that. You get a team and you come down here with your boys and play. You can be a cheerleader, too.' So we had them starting to come in. We got the reputation for starting girls' basketball in Alaska. The legislature sent me a nice commendation."

Eventually, with a boost from Title IX, and then the oil money that began rolling in from the Alaska pipeline, schools became wealthier and the Fairbanks and Anchorage schools expanded their girls' athletic programs. Sailors did do some teaching, mostly social studies and history, and overall enjoyed his time working at the school. Always in the back of his mind, though, was his primary goal of getting his guide business up and running in Alaska the way he had it going in Wyoming.

Also while at Glennallen, Sailors coached wrestling and track and field. In 1966, as part of the Glennallen American Legion Post, he started the Boys State Program which paralleled the program he worked with in Wyoming that sent high school students to the state capital to experience a weeklong insider view of the workings of the state legislature.

"Four or five years later when the pipeline came along they had money coming out of their ears," Sailors said. "Every little school in the state had a girls' team and a boys' team. We held a tournament in Glennallen with about nineteen teams in it and we won that. There was one in Palmer we should have won, but didn't. I think we won four or five state championships. Then I stopped coaching for years. I was just getting tired of it and I was putting more time into my guiding business. I had put my three years in as an assistant guide to Clco and started my own outfitting business."

For those who grew up in the lower forty-eight states it is a given that Wyoming and Montana are the two states that are most like Alaska, only with better highways. Alaska is bigger, more intense in its weather, and has even more plentiful offerings of big game and fish. It is the outdoors multiplied by a factor of five or ten.

In some ways the area where Sailors settled in Alaska is interchangeable with Wyoming. In Wyoming, he grew up and went to college in the shadows of the Snowy Mountain Range. In Alaska he could see the Wrangell–St. Elias Mountains from his land. Snow-coated Mount Sanford, at sixteen-thousand-plus feet, is the peak of greatest note in the range. On a clear day Mount Drum, more than twelve thousand feet in height, can be seen from the Glenn Highway near Glennallen. Kenny and Bokie described themselves to their Alaskan friends as a cowboy and cowgirl, but they also shared the traits of rural Alaskans who built their own homes.

Not only did Sailors set up his guide business—the 76 Ranch—overlooking the Gulkana River, just across the Richardson Highway and a short ways into the trees he cleared a little patch of land and built a small log cabin that in later years became their primary abode. Marilynne and Dan helped him build the main lodge where they could also put up visitors, but he pretty much built the small cabin by himself. It measured about thirty feet by twenty feet. There were moose antlers over the front door and although there was glass in the windows the structure resembled a cabin from pioneer days—small, sturdy, and homey. There were a few bedrooms of limited size and a kitchen where coffee was consumed at a hectic rate at the table. The closest neighbor was a quarter of a mile away, but in case of emergency, with Bokie's health being fragile, there was swift, easy access to the highway.

"It's a low-ceiling cabin," Sailors said of the smaller cabin that he built with his own hands and was still sturdy more than thirty years later. "That's to keep the heat in and it gets way below zero here in the winter. I'll tell you one thing: Those pro basketball players of today wouldn't be able to walk in the door without ducking. It wasn't built for a 7-footer. Even my brother Bud complained when he first came to visit. Bud hit his head on the doorjamb when he came in and said, 'Good gosh, Kenny, who did you build this house for, midgets?' Those logs have good staying power."

The community of Glennallen was in easy reach, but the forest, the river, and wildlife were even closer. Bokie went to work on the land adjacent to the smaller cabin and started a vegetable garden and a strawberry patch. Famed for her marksmanship early in life, she maintained her accuracy with a rifle she kept handy in case of animal intruders in the yard marauding through her personally landscaped food patches. You didn't want to make the feisty Bokie mad if you were a squirrel trying to work your way into the roof of the cabin, a moose trodding on the vegetables, or a black bear following his nose.

Once a black bear of some size strolled up to the cabin's back window and stood up straight. Bokie walked up to the window inside and rapped her knuckles hard against the glass, sending a message to the furry creature to skedaddle. "Get out of here!" was the firm response Bokie delivered to the bear, who had both size and strength on her and might well have been able to punch through the window if it had a mind to do so.

Grizzly bears could drop in, as well, although they were less frequent visitors. Sailors had been a basketball player and professional athlete for his entire youth, and guiding in the mountains in Wyoming kept him trim and in top shape. He led no less rigorous a life in Alaska. The flip side of the beauty of the land the Sailorses could gaze upon from their home was the harshness of it when there were attempts to explore it and guide on it by foot or horseback.

Much of Alaska is coastline and the best approach is by boat. Vast portions of the state's 586,000 square miles are inaccessible by road or boat and can only be reached by airplane. Although it stemmed from their accidental stopping place near Glennallen, the area where Sailors ended up living and using as his base of hunting operations, and his hunting camp itself, all encouraged the use of horses. The old cowboy was in his element in Alaska as much as he had been while living in Wyoming.

After moving to Gakona and establishing himself in Alaska following a three-year guide apprenticeship with Cleo McMahan, Sailors was once more in business as a guide and outfitter. The 76 Ranch was open for the hunting business and Sailors was back in the saddle again.

CHAPTER 15

Alaska Adventures

THE GRIZZLY BEAR THAT TURNED HIS HORSE into a nervous wreck is the most memorable bear that Kenny Sailors met in the Alaska wilderness. He has told the story many times because it remains vivid in his mind many, many years after the encounter took place. The event was notable because it was unexpected and because it was the only time he witnessed a particular horse behavior.

That is coming from a man who said he eventually thinks he spent more time in the saddle than Tom Mix and Roy Rogers combined. Sailors was never brandishing six-shooters, or posing for Hollywood cameras, but he rode his horses into the wild for years as part of his hunts. On this particular day Sailors was riding an old, dappled horse on a narrow trail in the Wrangell–St. Elias Mountains as he often did. He was riding alone, not in a pack string, and not with a hunter, and his mind was elsewhere. To the best of his recollection he was exploring for sheep.

"All of a sudden a large grizzly reared up on his hind legs from the brush with no warning," Sailors said. "I froze in the saddle. There was nowhere to go and nothing to do except wait. I held my breath and held everything motionless, feet in the stirrups, hands wrapped around the reins. I never saw him coming. He was hidden away off the trail. He stared at me and I stared at him and for a few seconds I wondered if he was going to charge. I wondered if I would become dinner for this huge, powerful, and menacing creature."

It was a reasonable fear. Although grizzly bears are often skittish around people, they are animals that behave in different ways depending on the circumstances. The Alaska grizzly might be eight feet tall and weigh a thousand-plus pounds. It has sharp teeth and sharper claws. While it might normally subsist on a diet of salmon and berries and ground squirrels and only rarely chows down on human beings, enough people-bear confrontations have been recorded to know that sometimes a bear will do the unexpected and attack. It might take only one swipe of its very sharp claws to kill a person.

Typically, bears do not go after people. But if a momma is protecting its young, all bets are off and no rules apply. They go into aggressive mode. Likewise, if a bear is surprised, caught off guard, it will leap up and perhaps charge. Sailors most likely surprised this bear. It may have been just coming out of a slumber, was snacking and didn't want to have its meal interrupted, or was simply not in the mood for company.

For someone who spent thirty-five years in Alaska and who spent more than fifty years guiding in Wyoming and Alaska Sailors was remarkably fortunate not to encounter the growling face of death in the wild when he was unable to defend himself or he wasn't prepared. This bear may have presented the greatest threat of his life and to his life.

"I remember that it was a clear, sunny, early fall afternoon," Sailors said, estimating that the event occurred sometime in the late 1970s. "We had the kind of clear, blue-sky day in Alaska that is a special gift from the Lord and that we don't get nearly often enough. If we did, I suppose, Alaska would have five million people, not 600,000. The rugged weather keeps folks away. My mind was on other things. It was a brushy area with plenty of cover. That's prime bear habitat. They tell you that when you're alone in the wilderness, in bear country, the best thing to do is sing, whistle, or tie a cowbell on your backpack if you're hiking, or if you're riding and you have a pack string to put a bell on one of the horses. In other words, make some noise to let the bear know you're there. If the bear knows you're coming, most likely he will just run away. You might not even know it was there. But if you're quiet and the wind is wrong, then you might sneak up on the bear and a surprised bear is usually an angry bear. Well, there I was on my horse, truly minding my own business, but too casual. I wasn't being as sharp as you should be."

Sometimes not even whistling "Dixie" or singing "Oh! Susanna," neither of which Sailors was doing as a bear distraction, helps anyway. This time he was just cruising along enjoying the sunshine when he should have been doing something to alert bears that he was in the neighborhood.

"The bear rose up about twenty-five yards ahead just off the trail," Sailors said. "It wasn't a huge one, but it was a nice-sized bear. They stand up to look at you because they don't have good eyesight. The bear was over six feet tall and weighed probably five hundred pounds. That's not a large grizzly, but really, though, it doesn't make much difference. A grizzly is a grizzly, whether he weighs five hundred pounds or a lot more. They all look big when they stand up like that. I was maybe 170 pounds at the time. I don't think anyone would have put us in the same weight class for a boxing match."

When the distance between a person and a bear is closer than the usual distance between them and their parked car, and there is nothing in-between, the person is usually thinking about just how huge that animal looks regardless of its actual weight.

"Any bear that you see up close looks very large," Sailors said. "Just ask anyone who's been in that situation. The only time a grizzly might look small is if he's on the other side of the bars at a zoo. I've always been amazed by grizzly bears' heads. The biggest ones I've ever seen are literally a couple of feet around. You know what that old boy's hat size must have been?"

Sailors was not about to pull out a tape measure and try to fit this grizzly for a Stetson, either, but worse for him, since he had been so loosey-goosey in his travels, he didn't have a rifle handy to pull out and fire, either. Bears being Olympic 100-meter-dash-finals swift, there is often no time for a quick draw and to get a shot off for protection.

"Bears have monstrous shoulders," Sailors said. "Imagine the biggest of professional football linemen with their pads and you still haven't approached the width of a bear's shoulders, nor have you really hinted at the power he's got. Their arms, or front legs, look as if they've spent a lifetime lifting weights in the gym, too. They're just very powerful beasts. The thing that scares you, though, is not so much the size alone, but the length of the claws. They're a couple of inches long and razor sharp. They look like a row of hooks."

Since Sailors never saw any cubs, he did not blame the aggressive look of the grizzly on a mother-and-child connection, but guessed that he had wakened the bear as it slept along the trail. The wind was blowing wrong for the bear to have sensed Sailors coming from very far away. He speculated that the bear had downed a belly full of blueberries and was sleeping off its pleasing meal.

"It will take a bear just a couple of seconds to go twenty-five yards," Sailors said. "They're so fast. So you're not safe at all at that distance. I never had time to get my rifle out from under my leg, or anything. He was so close and it happened so fast. He stood there and looked at me, I don't know how long. It seemed like an hour to me. That old bear, you could see hair standing up on his hump and he was clacking his teeth. I was just setting there looking at him. When a bear is clacking his teeth like that you tend to get worried. He's debating whether he's going to charge or not. If the intent of the bear is to scare you with those choppers I can tell you, it works."

Such stare downs may only last seconds, but be imprinted on a man's mind forever. They also may be the difference between life and death or being attacked and scarred forever. The bear threatened and Sailors watched.

"The only thing I had going for me—and it wasn't much really—was that I was on a horse," Sailors said. "We probably looked pretty big to him. The horse couldn't have turned on the trail very fast and it couldn't have outrun the bear from a standing start, but it gave me a slight feeling of confidence, as if I wasn't in this alone. I was real interested to see what this horse was going to do. It was a new horse. It had never been in the mountains before. He come out of the flat country and I don't think it had ever hunted before."

When it came to experience that horse might as well have just come off a job as a carousel horse. It certainly had not come upon a bear like this before. Sailors was focused on the bear, not the horse, though, for a while, and only after the entire scene seemed paralyzed for a moment did he realize that the horse under him was probably scared to death, terrified of moving, too frightened to do anything. The horse seemed to stretch its entire body out, actually getting a little bit longer. Sailors felt as if he was dropping in the saddle by six inches or a foot. This was the horse's physical reaction to flat-out fear of the bear.

"Then, all of a sudden, I felt the horse begin to shake, just tremble all over," Sailors said. "It was as if I was sitting on top of a small earthquake. He was shaking just like he had St. Vitus' dance. He was too scared to run, which is probably the best thing that could have happened. If he had started to run that bear might have taken us. That close, he'd have got us, I imagine. The whole thing probably only took twenty seconds and when the bear dropped down on all fours and disappeared back into the brush again I looked down for the first time. That horse I was on had broken out into a cold sweat. There was sweat all over his withers and his neck. He looked like he'd just run a mile and a half. He pretty near had a heart attack, I bet. I don't know what I looked like, but just as bad probably."

The bear lost interest in Sailors and his horse, deciding that they were no threat after all. The bear didn't feel like fighting and just wandered off, a bit huffy, perhaps, but no doubt satisfied it had defended its territory. That was as close as Sailors ever got to a bear that was in a foul mood and he knows he was fortunate to get away just with breaking into a sweat and not having anything worse happen. The horse had no comment on the situation, but Sailors was probably right that it came close to suffering a heart attack out of pure fright.

Later, Sailors wrote a poem based on the encounter called "King And The Griz." In part it reads,

The only time that I recall
I couldn't make him go
Was late one fall—twelve miles from camp
In about a foot of snow

A track came down a brushy gulch
And crossed in front of us
Old King just stopped—he wouldn't budge
His heart began to rush

Them tracks was like 'lectric fence
The fronts about eight inches wide
Old King just stood stiff-legged
With little shivers in his hide.

In the poem the rider climbs down from the horse and leads it out of the area on foot, though both the man and horse keep looking behind them in case the bear showed up.

The poem ends this way:

Well—back at camp Old King & I
Were glad the day was done
& to this day he still don't know
I wasn't even packin' my gun!

Sailors knew that most of the time a bear wanted no part of dealing with a person, but that didn't mean the situation wouldn't turn into the 5 percent that result in an assault or injury.

"You never know which time it's going to be," he said. "I know I never want to get into a staring contest with a grizzly like that again. Strange things can happen in the wilderness when you're out hunting. But the strangest of all is when you become the hunted."

There were many similarities and many differences between hunting and guiding in Wyoming and hunting and guiding in Alaska. There were elk in Wyoming and caribou in Alaska. There were black bears in Wyoming and both black bears and grizzly bears in Alaska. There were moose in both places, but the moose grew much larger in Alaska. There were sheep in both places and the elevation was higher for most sheep hunts in Wyoming, but both places involved mountain climbing. Alaska had ptarmigan and Wyoming had grouse. Most guides in Alaska don't use horses, but Sailors was able to transplant horseback riding from one place to the other. Many more guides use airplanes to transport their hunters to their camps in Alaska.

"Substituting horses for the airplane also deals with the whole issue of fair chase in advance," Sailors said. "There's no question of a violation when you're not even using an airplane. Flying and hunting the same day is unethical and illegal. Or even searching for game by plane, but that never comes up if you're using horses. Horses give hunters a better hunt. They have more fun and they have a broader experience in the wilderness."

Wyoming had its share of wind and blizzards, especially when riding up high at ten thousand feet of elevation, but Alaska definitely packed a more serious winter punch.

"Winter in Alaska was much more severe," Sailors said.

What he didn't know when he picked the Glennallen-Gakona area to settle in was that the winter lows could touch forty degrees below zero Fahrenheit. By any definition that is chilly.

Once Sailors got the 76 Ranch up and operating he and Marilynne missed out on some of those frigid temperatures by traveling through the lower forty-eight states in winter to drum up business. Starting in January and running for a couple of months, there is a long tradition of outdoor trade shows with regular spots on the calendar in many big cities across the United States. They are held in the off-season from fishing and hunting when guides would otherwise be idle. Instead, the guide-businessman travels from city to city and makes appearances at the big shows in Chicago, Detroit, Pennsylvania, and all across the Midwest and East.

"Marilynne and I would go to the sportsman shows and rent booths," Sailors said. "We always brought some antlers."

It was a little bit like show-and-tell. The antlers served as advertising for what a hunter who dreamed of hunting for a large moose might see. To many in the states Alaska was still somewhat of a mythological place, a hunting and fishing paradise that was wild and free and romantic. They saved their money for once-in-a-lifetime excursions. To some extent the same attitude prevails today that did so in the early 1970s when the Sailorses were on tour selling their ten-day hunting trips in the Wrangells.

"They seemed to be fascinated by Alaska," Sailors said. "This was a fun business, but it was hard work."

Sailors's partner was Cleo McMahan and both men had sons that wished to guide, as well. Two of McMahan's sons joined in over time and so did Dan Sailors.

"I worked for Pop in the guiding business," Dan Sailors said. "He was not active much in the fishing business. I started the fishing business on the Gulkana. "[Mom] pretty much worked on the paperwork. She didn't come to camp very much. Sometimes, but not often. She could hunt."

The name of the business was Alaska Wild Country Guides & Outfitters and it was easy to be seduced by the beautiful scenic pictures showcased on the brochure. If you went hunting with Kenny or Dan Sailors you were going to be riding horses into the backcountry and the high country of the Wrangell–St. Elias Mountains. There was also a fairly good chance you would see a bear sometime on the week-and-a-half-long hunt whether you wanted to or not.

"Bears are everything in the Wrangell–St. Elias Range," Sailors said. Which is why he thought one guide who boasted about never carrying a gun on his trips was a bit crazy and careless. It came back to haunt him. "Anyway, this guy made the statement to quite a few people about not carrying a gun. One summer day he was walking to his cabin, pack on his back, no gun. A bear looked up, saw him, and boom! That was it, right after him. There was no sweet-talking this bear. The bear didn't even raise up on her legs or anything. He showed up and she was after him.

"He said it was the first time in his life he realized he was in trouble and he shrugged out of that pack in a hurry. He ran for the first tree he could find,

Kenny Sailors loved to use horses on the trails into his hunting camps in Wyoming and Alaska. Here he is admiring the scenery in Alaska's Wrangell–St. Elias Mountains. (Photo courtesy Kenny Sailors.)

grabbed onto the trunk, then some branches, and was hauling himself up the tree when the bear got there. He didn't get up quite high enough and the bear took one swipe at his gluteus maximus. He finally got himself pulled up in that tree and he didn't have anything with him to scare that bear away. No gun, that's for sure. The bear stood up and started shaking that tree and he held on tight and dripped blood down on the bear. He was in the tree a long time given how he was bleeding. Finally, the bear gave up on him. He was able to climb down, get back to his car, and get to a hospital.

"I've never had to climb a tree myself and neither have any of my hunters. I've thought about it a few times, that I would have if I could have, but there were no trees around."

Sometimes the best and most appropriate shot at wildlife is from a still camera, or a video camera rather than a rifle.

"There was a time when we were out in my hunting camp in Alaska, in the Wrangells, where I tell people I could have put Walt Disney out of business if I had the photographic and sound equipment set up for it," Sailors said.

A young woman named Julie James, who had played on one of Sailors's basketball teams at Glennallen, was his camp cook. Usually, when the guide and hunters go into the field, the cook hangs around camp watching over things and preparing dinner when the hungry bunch returns. It was usually quiet at camp without anyone else around.

"One time I came riding into camp, packing a moose," Sailors said. "I was unloading and getting the moose off the horses and up onto some logs we had there to keep it off the ground and she yells, 'Coach! Look over there!' There was a grizzly sow and two cubs coming down off the hill. They were at the end of the lake, not more than four hundred yards away. There was a hollow place that we had dug out a little bit outside of the camp in order to put meat scraps in. I didn't want to have them in camp because that would draw bears to us. We just dumped it away from camp and stuff usually got eaten up by birds and animals. The sow ambled on in with these fairly young cubs and settled in on the pit. They were close enough that we could hear and see everything with the naked eye. We didn't even need field glasses. They were all cozy in the pit, munching everything up. It was a free lunch for them with no work. They had to love that. And then all of a sudden Julie yells once again at me: 'Look! Here comes another one!'

"Sure enough, another grizzly was headed towards the scrap pile. Immediately, I thought, 'There's going to be some trouble.' I went and got the binoculars then and I could see from the way he was moving that it was a big, old boar. He could tell right where to come by that scene. He was coming to the garbage. I said to Julie, 'We're going to see some fun here in a minute. Something's going to happen.'"

Not all animal lovers realize that large, male grizzly bears will kill cubs and devour them if they get the chance. Mother bears know that the boars are not friends of the family, though. Sailors said he thought a huge wrestling match was about to ensue, something that would put Dusty Rhodes and Hulk Hogan to shame. Unlike Sailors and Julie, the mother bear did not see the approach of the boar. The moment the momma bear spotted the boar she barked commands at the cubs to get the heck out of there and then in another instant erupted and zoomed at the big bear.

"She took off after the boar and they swatted each other and clacked at each other," Sailors said, "and they growled all over that hillside for a few minutes. When they were fighting there was a lot of noise, a lot of confusion, and they were really popping each other. When they hit each other with those forepaws, boy, oh boy. Those crazy little cubs, though, didn't listen to their mother. They were just kind of setting there watching the whole affair. Mom was able to run that bigger bear off. A sow's vicious when she's got cubs and she really worked him over. He ran away and she trailed him for a while to make sure he was really going. She wasn't taking any chances at all."

Once the area was clear of danger momma bear galloped back to her cubs and while she may have expected them to heed her warning and to scamper up a tree, she discovered that they had remained exposed in the open and paid no attention to her advice.

"When you watch a bear run on all fours it's as if they're all shoulders," Sailors said. "Their shoulders are rotating and moving with each step and you really get a sense of their power. Well, she got back to the cubs and the first thing she did was go up to one of the cubs, who didn't have any idea what was coming, and she swatted him! She must have knocked him twenty feet. You should have seen that cub dash for the first tree he could find then. The other one had already gotten the message and was up a tree. I think momma made her feelings clear. I bet those cubs listened to her the next time she told them to do something.

"Walt Disney really would have been jealous if we had that all on film footage. It would have been an Academy Award winner."

One way horses were very useful on Wrangell–St. Elias hunts were as meat packers once a hunter scored a successful kill. Sometimes Sailors and his assistants would pack a horse with the meat after the moose was gutted and he made a solo trek back to his ranch with it as the assistant guide took the hunters to another spot so a second shooter in the group might get his chance.

The only problem with traveling alone, as Sailors had already discovered when riding on a narrow trail, was that he didn't make much noise and so if he came upon a bear it could be an unpleasant unplanned meeting.

"One time a moose hunt almost got me into major-league trouble with a grizzly bear," Sailors said. "I was riding along this narrow trail [instant replay], a game trail used by bear and moose that had overgrown brush and vegetation. I rode my horse down in a draw and was halfway up the other side when a grizzly cub came over the top. Then, another one. You know, of course, that the mother can't be far behind in a situation like that and sure enough the sow came over the top next. The bears were no more than forty yards away.

"All three of them reared up on their hind legs, little ones imitating momma and stood there looking at me. I remember it clearly, and it sounds funny, but it isn't anything to laugh about when you're there. Momma was not pleased. She stood up clacking her teeth, the hair standing up on her back. Fortunately, the old mare I was riding was a veteran. She had been out hunting a lot and had run across bears before. So she didn't bolt. That was a good thing because it might have incited the sow into chasing me."

What concerned Sailors was what the little cubs were going to do. They had no experience confronting a man on a horse and they were curious about everything. If they had moved toward him the mother bear would have felt compelled to come after him as a way of shielding them from harm.

"They lowered themselves to all fours and they started moving towards me," Sailors said. "Then they stood up again and stared at me. The sow was barking at them a little, making noises, grunting at them. She didn't like the situation. You could tell she was telling them to stay put, to come back by her side. I was worried they were going to bring her right to me. She turned off to the side a little bit and waited for them. I started talking to them in a normal voice, steady, quiet. I said, 'Go on, get out, you little stinkers. Go to your momma.' They had me talking for quite a spell. I was hoping to keep her calm, too. I must be a sweet-talkin' guy because after listening to me for a while they turned around and ambled into the trees. Maybe I just bored them."

Kids, they just don't listen.

Bears were a nuisance and threat during Alaska hunts for other species. They often got in the way and were more dangerous to humans than the animals they were hunting. Bears were also always on the prowl for a free meal if a person shot a moose or caribou. A bear would have no qualms about claiming the carcass for its own. One thing Sailors wished to avoid, above all, though, was a bear terrorizing his horses while they were in camp.

While the hunters were out in the field, the horses would be tied up in camp. If a bear came after them they could be vulnerable and trapped. One day the nightmare scenario played out while Sailors was guiding two brothers from Michigan in the Wrangells. They were in the mountains miles above camp and he was sweeping the area with his binoculars. He saw a bear in the distance, but realized that if it stayed on its current course it would show up in hunting camp.

"When you tie up your horses in the wilderness, you tie them up tight enough to hold, but not so tight they can't break loose if they really need to," Sailors said. "If they're trained and good hunting horses they won't break the rope. We tied them up with a half-inch hemp rope. But if they were frightened and in a tense situation they could snap that rope in a second and free themselves to run. A big horse has the strength to do that, especially if his adrenaline is up. A bear coming toward him would get it up quick."

Of course that would mean the horses would scatter like leaves on the wind and the hunters might have a long hunt. It also meant that a terrified horse on the loose could severely injure itself, break a leg, and have to be put down.

"The bear was headed in their direction and if he spotted the horses and surprised them, chances were that he would jump one of them," Sailors said. "But even if he didn't get one of the horses he would definitely scare them and they'd break loose and we would have a long walk. I clued the hunters in to what was happening and hustled down off the mountain to see if I could get to the horses before the bear did. I slid down the rocks, rushed through the brush, and I got down to the creek bottom between the bear and the horses. The bear was taking his time. He was munching on berries as he came, but he was still headed in our direction."

Sailors pondered the situation and tried to figure out the best way to divert the bear away from camp and the horses with the smallest risk to his own well-being. He thought a little bit like a basketball player when he devised his plan.

"I decided the best defense would be a good offense and I'd try to spook him out of the area," Sailors said. "I didn't even have a rifle with me. I left it under a tarp near the horses so I could have it handy when I came back. So I threw some rocks at the bear to get his attention. The rocks landed near him and he wheeled around to see where the noise was coming from. But the bear didn't see anything. He looked and didn't see me, so he continued on his way."

So much for Plan A. Sailors went to Plan B with a fresh idea for diverting the bear off his moseying-along path. By then Sailors was very close to the horses.

"So I yelled at him," Sailors said. "I don't know what that sounds like to a bear, a human hollering. But he stopped and turned around and took a few steps back to where I was. Then he raised up on his hind legs for a better view, looking in my direction. I suppose by then he spotted me, though I was quite a ways away. As long as I kept yelling at the bear he was curious. It must have sounded like something he didn't like or wasn't familiar with. As soon as I shut up and kept quiet, he ambled away. I stayed with the horses. I guess that was a pretty dumb thing to do not having the gun with me. I couldn't have shot the bear if he'd come at me. I've learned since that you would be just as well off not yelling. The bear probably would have passed the horses by anyway."

As any hunter of big game in North America or Africa will say, the most dangerous situation to be faced is when a hunter wounds an animal, but it doesn't go down and leaves a trail of blood that must be followed into tall grass or other cover. The humane thing to do is put the animal out of its misery. The only way to stop it from escaping is to track it down and fire another shot to finish it.

However, the process can be hair-raising. Many times the animal will crawl away and stop under cover just to rest because it has been weakened by the first bullet. It may be simply waiting for its attacker to come near him to exact revenge. A wounded lion or Cape buffalo in Africa, or a bear in Alaska, can be lethal to someone searching for it.

"If that bear wasn't angry at you before, you can bet he's howling and mad and vicious with a gunshot wound," Sailors said. "In all my years of guiding I only went into the brush after an injured bear once. This was in my early years as a guide. You can't really let them get away, however, because they'll be very dangerous to other hunters in the area. It's the obligation of the guide, if a hunter isn't able to finish the bear off. You've got to do it.

"If the brush is thick, or it's getting dark, wait until the next day. And sometimes that's a good idea anyway because he may die by then. The bear was bleeding a lot and I could track him. And even though he was in the thick stuff I could see him before I stumbled on him. It's the scariest thing in the world when you know a bear is lying quietly in the thickets. The sweat is pouring off of your head and all kinds of thoughts go through your mind. With a bear's speed and strength, one whack with that forepaw and it's all over. They can pulverize you before you can react. That's the kind of thing that goes through your mind when you're tracking bear. Every terrifying story you've ever heard. Your next step can result in death. I was very fortunate. My bear was dead when I found him."

Sailors's son, Dan, adopted the same type of prudence his father showed in the wilderness. Once a hunter took a shot at a bear and was certain he had hit it. He and his friends tried to convince the younger Sailors to go into the brush to finish it off. Dan surveyed the situation and said, "No way." It was a good thing. The bear had not even been wounded. It would have been waiting for him under cover at full strength.

"The guide has got to be smarter," Kenny Sailors said. "He's got to use patience. Patience is very important to safety. You also can't let a hunter talk you into something. You're the one who's the expert. You're the one being paid to exercise good judgment."

Sailors said two guide friends of his were killed by bears over the years while he was guiding in Alaska.

Once Sailors and an assistant guide had to compete with a bear for a moose that one of their hunters had shot just before dusk and didn't have enough time to quarter and cape before darkness fell. They knew they would have to get an early start the next morning because the assistant had seen bear sign all over the area and was sure a bear was going to seize upon the left-behind carcass for a free meal.

"Even before we got in sight of the dead moose we got a hint there was a bear on it," Sailors said. "The horses started acting up. They were balking as if they didn't want to go on and they started to snort. Sure enough there was a grizzly bear. I had a twelve-gauge shotgun, with double-ought buck with me. You need firepower when you're going into those circumstances."

The grizzly on the moose carcass was a young one and when Sailors and his assistant Harley threw things on it the bear retreated more readily than it might have if it was an adult.

"The bear didn't go very far, though," Sailors said. "He only went into the trees about fifty yards away. I stood shotgun, literally, like I was guarding the gold on an old West stagecoach while Harley bent over the moose and went to start caping it out. It turned out the meat was ruined. It had dirt all over it and the bear chewed off one ear of the cape. While Harley was working I could hear the bear circling in the timber. First you'd hear him to the right. Then you'd hear him behind you. It was creepy, especially in such a confined space. You didn't know what he'd do next. This went on for a good forty minutes."

Sailors and his assistant hauled out the horns, upper jaw cape, and the skull for a mount. The hunter didn't even mind the chewed-off ear. It just made the story a better one to tell his friends back home.

Periodically, Alaska is going to remind people that it is Alaska and deliver an early winter surprise. On one September 1, decades into Sailors's guiding career, he and a quartet of hunters were in their tents at camp in the Wrangell–St. Elias Range when it began to snow after dinner.

"Big, fat flakes," Sailors said. "And it kept falling. By midnight the tents were sagging from the weight of it. I was worried that every ridgepole we had was going to bust and fall in, including the cook tent. I got the guides up and we all went out in the slushy snow and started knocking it off the tents. One storage tent did break down. The next morning, when we woke up, we were in the middle of a regular winter storm. There was probably two feet of snow on the ground and it was still coming. It had gotten colder, too. Now I couldn't believe it. A little bit of snow was one thing, but a blizzard in September was a little bit premature. Well, we couldn't go out hunting in that kind of weather. It wasn't safe. We weren't the post office so we didn't have to deliver the mail that day."

The Sailors guide operation put everything on hold, heated up a lot of coffee, and passed out Louis L'Amour westerns—Sailors's favorite author—for everybody to read and pass the time. The only thing was that it didn't stop snowing after a day, or after two days. It snowed for the better part of a week on a scheduled ten-day hunt and the hunters were not happy campers, but very edgy. They even stated arguing over the L'Amour novels and whose turn it was to read what.

It took until the ninth day of the hunt for the skies to clear, so Sailors threw in a bonus day.

"The hunters got to worrying about how they were ever going to get out of the Wrangells and get back home," Sailors said. "For a while there they even forgot about the hunt. They were starting to think they'd be trapped there all winter."

The hunters finally got in some hunting on their hunting trip and almost miraculously over that squeezed-together two-day period of activity following the snow everything broke just right. Every single one of them got a sheep and didn't even have to climb a mountain to do so. The sheep had descended from their mountainous perch to a nearby valley.

"In those two days you never saw such hunting in your life," Sailors said.

It beat going home with a souvenir snowball from the freak storm Alaska threw at them.

CHAPTER 16

Back to Basketball in Alaska

ALTHOUGH KENNY SAILORS RETIRED FROM high-level competitive basketball by hanging up his sneakers following his fifth year in the NBA, he never actually stopped playing the game. Wherever he was living he might wander over to a nearby gym and take some jump shots. He might play one-on-one games with whomever was around.

Much later in life Sailors played one-on-one against his grandchildren. He was in his sixties, but never lost to them. He might fool around with the ball during the period when he coached the Glennallen girls' and boys' teams. After all, he was already in a gym. Once he finished his coaching stint in Glennallen Sailors figured that was it for him and basketball in any kind of serious way. He was just like any other Joe Fan, watching college games and NBA games on TV in his living room.

Until the late 1980s, that is, when out of nowhere an offer came for him and Bokie to sample another portion of the state that was also very rural and very small. The call came from Angoon, Alaska, on Admiralty Island. The island, located in the Southeast section of the state, not far from Juneau, the state capital, was often referred to as a place that had more bears than people living there.

The people that ran the Angoon schools wanted to know if Sailors would like to coach the girls' basketball team at the high school and teach a little bit. At the time Sailors was sixty-seven years old and his body was slowing down in terms of leading hunts. Dan was more or less in control of the business. He and Bokie talked it over and committed to giving it a try. Sailors said he was really going in order to scout additional bear hunting grounds, but then he admitted it was good to try something new as you got older so a person didn't stagnate.

Alaska is so vast that from one tip of the state to the other measures more than fifteen-hundred miles (and that doesn't involve the Aleutians). Gakona to Admiralty Island were not quite that far apart, but it was at least a thousand miles and you couldn't drive there. In the two-plus decades since Sailors helped found the girls' basketball team at Glennallen high school, basketball had spread like a forest fire throughout the state, becoming the most popular sport for girls and boys even in the smallest of communities. The tiny schools with enrollments of fifty or so students couldn't hope to field a football or hockey team, but you only needed five to play basketball.

In 1988, Sailors was coaching the Angoon girls' basketball team for a second season. He was sixty-eight and he and Bokie were living another adventure in rural Alaska. The six hundred residents of Angoon were mostly Tlingit Indians and there were just thirty-seven students in the grades nine-through-twelve high school. Yet Sailors had fifteen girls on his team.

Imagine what the players thought in this basketball-crazed town when they heard that a former NBA player was moving to Angoon to coach them.

"At first it was 'A Boston Celtics player? Here? What?'" said player Michelle Howard, a 6-foot-2 player whom Sailors nicknamed "Big Girl." "But he doesn't talk about it. Only when you ask. It was kind of neat to see. Last year when we got to different towns, people asked for his autograph."

Once in a while, often when nobody else was around, Sailors might stretch and take a few jump shots in the gym. Same old form, if not the same vertical leap that he displayed about fifty years earlier at the University of Wyoming.

"I bet I scored a thousand points off this one shot alone," Sailors said of his jumper.

The point in Angoon, however, was not for Sailors to make jump shots, but to teach his players how to make them with more accuracy. There was not a conceited bone in Sailors's body and he realized that to this generation he was just an old-timer. His job was to teach and coach, to impart lessons, not to show off. Coaching at a tiny school, where the basic mode of transportation to play against schools from other small schools in Southeast Alaska was by Alaska Marine Highway, the ferry. The travel is long and the stays for road games are not a few hours and out. The ferry ride to Kake took sixteen and a half hours and the team stayed for games played on two days, sleeping on the gym floor in sleeping bags, a common occurrence in Bush Alaska.

There was a great passion for basketball in Angoon and on game nights in the winter, when the weather was frequently dismal (though more rain than snow fell in the area) the best live action in town was at the gym. Everyone who was able went to the games and packed the hall.

Sailors formed a bond with other educators and coaches at the school and showed off the lighter side of his personality as he, principal Ronald Gleason, athletic director Rick Anderson, and boys' basketball coach Bill Noonkesser teased one another and made jokes at each other's expense, usually outside of hearing distance of the teenagers.

"It's a good place to coach," Sailors said. "Everybody's gung-ho about basketball, the parents, the teachers." And then he was interrupted by Anderson. "But they don't know the rules. That's how Sailors can buffalo everyone."

Added Noonkesser, "He's the ugliest coach I've ever worked with." That dig made Sailors whoop with laughter.

The head honchos at the school quickly took a shine to Sailors. He was self-effacing, not swelled-headed, and while they didn't know in advance what to make of a former NBA player moving to Angoon, he was quickly adopted and became prized in the community.

"He's considered a treasure," Gleason said in a serious moment when he wasn't busy insulting Sailors or making fun of him. Then he really poured on the compliments. "Occasionally, you're exposed to genius. If you're lucky enough you can share in that genius. He's a role model. He embodies what you want athletes to do. He's a self-made athlete. He embodies discipline, initiative, dedication, perseverance, sportsmanship, and citizenship."

If Sailors listened to that in great detail he would have been blushing brighter red than any skin tone received from sunburn.

Sailors was a solo coach. He did not have an assistant coach or a team manager. When practices were called for later in the day after school, or at any odd times, the players were let into the gym when the coach arrived bearing the key. At the time Angoon played in AA competition, the second-smallest classification. Ironically, during Sailors's first year leading the Eaglettes, his small team was supported by cheerleaders. During the 1988–89 season, his second, there were no cheerleaders. They all decided from what they saw that it would be more fun to play basketball under Coach Sailors, who led his first squad to a 20–5 record.

One of Sailors's coaching traits was to make every aspect of practice a competition pitting the players against one another, from sprints to keeping score in scrimmages. Sometimes he bought soft drinks for the winners. Sailors got his points across with firm instruction, but he was not a coach who screamed at his players.

Denise Starr, one of those players, said, "He doesn't ever yell. Unless we don't pay attention."

The players didn't really know what to make of Sailors's background in the sport and what they heard about him. They were eager to play for him and win and thought highly of how he treated them. But he was a senior citizen and they couldn't really envision him dashing up and down the court as a younger man in short pants.

"They think I'm too old to play," Sailors said. He punctuated that sentence by making a fifteen-foot jump shot.

During their time in Angoon Sailors and Marilynne lived in an apartment overlooking Chatham Strait. They did not give up their home in Gakona. The view from the window allowed them to look out on whales, eagles, and bears— those ever-present Alaska bears.

Admiralty Island was densely populated with bears and they tended to congregate at the town dump at the edge of town. It was wise to be prepared for bear sightings on short notice. One of the things Sailors used for conditioning for his girls' team, though, was long runs. That inevitably took them near the dump on the small number of paved roads. The same was true for the school's cross-country runners. Given his longtime guiding experience, Sailors was well aware that bears could present a problem, so when he sent the basketball team out for a run, or the distance runners, he accompanied them at the wheel of a pickup truck with a shotgun on his lap. Usually, the phrase "riding shotgun" in a vehicle refers to the rider in the passenger seat in charge of the radio. In this role, the coach was literally riding shotgun. He never had to fire to protect his players, though.

It was during this period of living in Angoon that Marilynne expressed a desire to one day spend winters in the dry heat of the desert Southwest. That would also offer a new experience that she hadn't tried.

"We're going to Arizona to hunt rattlesnakes," she said.

The first reaction was to think she was kidding, but Bokie was not fooling around on that topic. She meant it.

Sailors coached in Angoon to the end of the 1990–91 season when he turned seventy. Then he was faced with Alaska's mandatory retirement law and he accepted the ruling and he and Bokie moved back to Gakona. Not before coaching Jaeleen Kookesh, though, one of his favorite players, who always stayed in touch, and later became a lawyer. And not before coaching Angoon to a regional championship in 1990, a year the Eaglettes finished 19–5 and placed fourth in the state.

When Sailors announced his retirement from the school and his plan to return to Gakona, officials at Angoon prepared a glowing testimonial to send him off. The proclamation of appreciation (and part roast) read in part:

"This humble, lovable, former NBA star came to Angoon High School three years ago and has done tremendous things for our school.

"A. Kenny has done a tremendous job coaching. He has done what no one else could do. He took a bunch of girls under his wings and turned them into basketball players. Great job Kenny.

"B. Kenny has always been willing to help out. If a coach was sick or something, Kenny was right there. He helped out with track, cross-country, and boys' basketball practices on many occasions.

"C. He has done such things as be a dump guard during cross-country practices and meets. That old sawed-off shotgun, along with his Queen of the Dump—wife Bokie.

"D. I think we have all been amazed at Kenny's physical condition and athletic ability. Those of you who have arm-wrestled Kenny or played him on the basketball court know what I'm talking about. I can't image what you were like forty years ago.

"E. As for his classroom teaching, he did an outstanding job there, too, when he was conscious.

"F. The thing that stands out most about Kenny (and his wife Bokie) is that they have been two of the nicest, most gracious people we have ever met.

"G. On behalf of Angoon High School, best of luck. We'll miss you. Remember, in every life some rain must fall, a little hail, and that ain't all."

Sailors was also presented with a special picture and a plaque.

Sailors did little to promote himself if it wasn't for the guiding

The Angoon High School girls' basketball team coached by Kenny Sailors came in fourth in the 1990 state championships. (Photo courtesy Kenny Sailors.)

business, and did not travel in mainstream circles of college basketball for decades, so he essentially fell off the grid in the world of sports. He stayed in touch a little bit with old Wyoming friends, but not so much with former basketball teammates. One by one his college mates died off. One by one his former pro teammates passed away. Sailors did not attend college games and for many years his only connection to the sport was watching games on television. He admitted that he had been pretty much forgotten by the basketball world and was sure that many who watched him play years earlier thought he probably died.

Then came a major surprise and one that jump-started fresh awareness about Sailors, the jump shot, and his Wyoming team's achievements. In 1990, the NCAA came to Denver for the Final Four and in association with the games a special "Salute to Rocky Mountain Basketball" was held. It was a grand banquet and the organizers took some pains to locate Sailors in Angoon, and not only fly him to Denver for the events and the games while putting him up in a four-star hotel, they anointed him as the keynote speaker for the dinner.

All of a sudden Sailors was back in the news, back in the limelight, and sought after by sportswriters from around the country to tell his story. He was sixty-nine and quite spry, down-to-earth in his speech and he had a fascinating tale to tell. Many of Sailors's Cowboy teammates from the 1943 championship team had passed away over the preceding forty-seven years, but one who was in attendance for the festivities was Jim Reese.

Reese marveled at Sailors's top condition, learned he was still shooting some hoops while coaching, and said, "Haven't you ever heard of checkers? Or golf?"

Denver was one place that just about everyone heard of Sailors, though. The accompanying exhibits about the past days of college basketball in the region flattered Sailors taking his jump shot, dribbling up the court, and helping Wyoming to all of those wins. Some of the pictures seemed taller than Sailors's 5-foot-11.

Lest anyone overlook where Sailors was currently living, though, his wardrobe was an advertisement for his girls' basketball team. He wore a jacket that had the writing "Angoon, The Basketball Capital Of Admiralty Island" stitched on it. The jacket was a gift from his players. He was floored by the present, but not left flat-footed. That would be unseemly for the man who invented the jump shot.

It was quite the big deal dinner, attended by about twelve hundred basketball supporters, including former President Gerald Ford. Sailors and Reese, neither of whom attended any other NCAA title game previously beyond the one they played in, each spoke, and got some laughs.

"There've been a few changes," Sailors said of the NCAA's progression since he played in the tournament. "When a bunch of old guys like Jim Reese and I get together we talk about who set a pick for who. We can remember a lot of details, but when we walk out of here, we can't find our cars."

At 5-foot-8, Reese was shorter than Sailors, but if someone was silly enough to ask what position he played he answered deadpan, saying, "It's very obvious. I played the post—until they moved me to power forward."

Sailors was recognized walking down the street. He was recognized standing next to photos of him playing ball years earlier. He was recognized in the Marriott City Center. Everywhere he went for days leading up to the dinner and the games fans approached and wanted to shake his hand. Probably not a single one of them knew where Angoon, Alaska, was. He would have something to tell his girls when he went back there.

The attention was a bit surprising for Sailors, if only because he had not hung out with basketball crowds for years. He was proud of Wyoming's and his accomplishments, but he had lived a couple of lifetimes since, in Wyoming and in Alaska.

"You know," he said, "we never thought it was that big a deal. But I guess it is a big deal."

After their Angoon intermission, Kenny and Bokie returned to their cabin in Gakona and resumed their life in the Alaska wilderness. But the buzz surrounding Sailors did not subside. Once Sailors had thrust himself back into the headlines of college basketball as the University of Nevada Las Vegas won the crown, he did not completely retreat to obscurity.

By playing five seasons in the NBA Sailors had earned enough work credit to be vested in the league's pension play. He was also awarded extra time on his pension because of service during World War II. In 1991, in connection with the hundredth anniversary of the invention of basketball by James Naismith, the newly formed Basketball Alumni Foundation began lobbying for increased pensions for the early pioneers of the league. Originally, Sailors's pension was very small, but it eventually grew.

Sailors was selected as one of the "100 Greatest Players of the First Century of Basketball," and the foundation, which began with Boston Celtics legend Bill Russell as president, cut a deal with a marketing group to produce a set of basketball cards to raise money for the players. Russell sent a letter to Sailors and the other players to gain their support for the foundation. The letter stated in part, "The foundation was created with the primary goal of assisting former players, referees, and team personnel and/or their dependents in need of discreet financial assistance. Some may be in need because they were involved in the league prior to the adoption of the pension plan or because they have fallen on hard times. Whatever the circumstances, there are those who need our help."

Over the years the league grew more visible—especially internationally through the Dream Team that included Larry Bird, Michael Jordan, Magic Johnson, Charles Barkley, and so many other prominent stars representing the United States in the 1992 Summer Olympics in Barcelona—and the sport was on the cusp of a worldwide explosion that continues today. Sailors did realize a bump in his pension, though he was not in any type of serious financial straits, but the boom in basketball means that even the lowest paid player in the league now makes a half million dollars a season.

Whether it was in Angoon, or mostly in Gakona, at first, basketball fans and historians seemed capable of finding Sailors. Sailors appeared on only a couple of basketball cards during his career, but some collectors had them and wanted them autographed. Whether it was on a card, a photo, or just on a blank card, many sought Sailors's autograph. He was surprised when the attention ratcheted up.

"I get letters all the time," Sailors said. "A letter a day, sometimes more."

Sailors talked to sportswriters from *Sports Illustrated*, his local *Copper River Journal*, the *Anchorage Daily News*, the *Los Angeles Times*, the *New York Times*, the Associated Press, the *Arizona Republic*. Whenever he was able to retrieve copies of the story that came out he and Bokie saved them in a scrapbook. The *Old Farmer's Almanac* wrote about Kenny. Authors of magazine articles and books about firsts, inventions, or creativity in the development of sports contacted Sailors for a chat.

He had been rediscovered, with a vengeance, after his appearance in Denver in 1990. Maybe because Alaska was a little bit more accessible by then than it was when he and Bokie drove that dusty highway in 1965. It was nice to be remembered. It was nice to get some fresh recognition. It was nice to be acknowledged for his contribution to the game through the innovation of the jump shot.

A group of old friends began lobbying to get Sailors into the Naismith Basketball Hall of Fame in Springfield, Massachusetts. They wrote letters on his behalf, drummed up some favorable commentary from aging coaches.

"I'd like to see Coach in the Hall of Fame," Bokie said. "I think he deserves it."

Sailors did not get too wrapped up in that process and the call never came to beckon him for induction into the sport's main Hall of Fame. However, Sailors had not embraced either golf or checkers. He was not anywhere close to being sedentary when he completed his tenure in Angoon.

"I've got two or three good jumps left in me," he said.

CHAPTER 17

Return to Wyoming

KENNY SAILORS DIDN'T SEE THE NEXT STAGE of his life coming at all. It was like being blind-sided, having your jump shot blocked by a 7-footer that you never even sensed was in the neighborhood. Kenny and Marilynne were still in Alaska when the new millennium arrived and they planned to stay in Alaska for the rest of their lives.

By 2000 Kenny and Bokie had been living in Alaska for thirty-five years. For decades Bokie had coped with emphysema and by the 1990s she had an oxygen tank on call at the little cabin in Gakona.

"The doctors didn't think she'd live to be fifty," Sailors said. "I think that outdoors lifestyle helped keep her going. She outlived that prognosis by a good one-third."

However, as the new century was dawning Marilynne appeared to be developing some new health problems. One thing Alaskans revel in as a perk of living in the state is the extravagant light shows they are periodically blessed with in the night sky—the northern lights. Some Alaskans even have phone trees so that when the lights glitter and wave they call friends and tell them to look outside. Since the Sailorses didn't have a neighbor inside a half mile they simply took advantage of those sights by themselves.

"She loved to go out and watch the northern lights and so did I," Sailors said, "especially when they come down right around you. You can always hear a couple of old owls hooting at each other off in the distance or you could hear a pack of wolves yapping. She loved that and so did I. We used to stand out there, even in cold weather, even in our pajamas."

One night when the northern lights were out and the wolves were howling the Sailorses had been admiring the night sky. Then they went inside. Kenny went to sleep, but when he woke up he realized that Bokie was not in the bedroom and was not in the cabin. He found her outside in the dark, oblivious to the cold, wearing just a thin kimono-type nightgown. That's when he realized something might be wrong.

Doctors concluded that Marilynne was suffering from Alzheimer's, and was in a certain stage of dementia. The doctors also advised that living in a remote cabin where she could easily disappear in the woods was too risky and told Sailors, "Kenny, you've got to get her out of here or you're going to lose her. She's going to wander off and freeze to death."

Sailors said he initially investigated the possibility of some proper senior medical living facilities in Anchorage and Fairbanks, but that there was a waiting list in each location and he believed the circumstances were closer to an emergency. Sailors's daughter, Linda, was living in Idaho and she invited her parents to stay with her. "Come on down, I'll help you, Dad," Linda said, and so they moved to her place in Gooding, Idaho, for a little while.

Bokie's condition worsened and eventually doctors told Kenny that she belonged in a place with highly skilled nursing care.

"We didn't want to put her in a nursing home," he said, "but we found a big place with mostly women in it and I talked to the nurses. It was an assisted living facility. She never did get that bad where she didn't know me. She didn't know some people, even some of her grandkids, but she always remembered who I was."

Marilynne died in 2002 at the age of seventy-nine. While she was suffering from dementia that was not the true cause of death, Sailors said. "The breathing, the emphysema is what killed her. She couldn't control it like she had before she got dementia."

At that point Sailors had been out of Alaska for a couple of years and he ended up returning to another old favorite place—Laramie—site of his great athletic triumphs in college.

"I'd lived in Laramie longer than anyplace in Wyoming," Sailors said. "I went to high school here and went to college here. I met my wife here at the university and went into the Marines and came back. Both of my kids were born here, so I was kind of familiar with Laramie. I like Laramie. I like the people here. It never has gotten too big. Marilynne loved it. She loved it here. But she loved it better up there in Alaska. So did I."

After Kenny and Bokie left Gakona, their small cabin was sold, but the 76 Ranch stayed in the family. Dan ran the guiding business for a while, but eventually tired of it. He and his wife, Jeanne, moved to the village of Aniak where he runs a flight service and works for the Alaska Department of Fish and Game. One of Dan's daughters, Kelly, her husband, Chad, and their family reside on the 76 Ranch property in Gakona, though they are not guiding out of it.

Into his eighties, periodically Kenny returned to Gakona for visits and sometimes to hunt. "I went back hunting moose," Sailors said. "I drove up and brought a freezer and filled it up with meat."

Alaska will always be part of Kenny Sailors's makeup, but quite surprising to him when he moved back to Laramie, he learned how well-remembered his basketball exploits were and how grateful his university was for what he did as captain of the team that won the NCAA crown in 1943.

The magnitude of becoming an NCAA men's basketball champion grew over the years, increased in value. The title gained more and more luster as the nation gained more and more appreciation for college basketball and the challenge of winning such a crown. In Laramie, at the University of Wyoming, Sailors was living history. As time passed, too, he also became the last living link to that glorious history. After Floyd Volker and Jim Reese passed away, Sailors was the last surviving member of the 1942–43 Cowboy team. And there he was, living right in town, living just blocks from the Arena-Auditorium, or the "Double A," as folks in Laramie like to call it. That building houses and displays the trophies that Sailors and his teammates won.

With the death of Marilynne, Sailors had just lost his life partner after fifty-nine years of marriage, but in Laramie he found an extended family that loved him and treated him like a king. The late-in-life recognition actually began to envelop Sailors while he was still living in Alaska. The Rocky Mountain salute dinner in 1990 at the Final Four in Denver was one example.

In 1993 Wyoming created its own university sports Hall of Fame and Kenny Sailors was selected for and inducted with the first class. The Arena-Auditorium is a circular building and displayed on the walls as one walks around the structure are pictures and words describing the achievements of the inductees. Sailors is basically first in line and the ironic thing is that he often walks past his own homage without glancing at it. That's because Sailors regularly uses the hallway surrounding the seats and courts as a workout venue.

A 1993, fiftieth anniversary reunion with surviving members of the 1942–43 championship team. Kenny Sailors is third from the left. (Photo courtesy the University of Wyoming.)

On the days of inclement weather he takes his constitutional by walking laps around the inside of the building. It may be raining or sleeting outside, but Sailors keeps up his good-faith efforts to stay in shape. He may have lost his vertical leap to age (he jokes it is down from a likely thirty-six inches to three inches), but he still works at trying to stay somewhat trim and healthy by walking a mile or two.

The first class in the Hall of Fame was inducted on October 29, 1993, and essentially Sailors was inducted twice. He was chosen for his individual exploits on the court and also selected was the 1942–43 Cowboy basketball team that won the NCAA championship.

When it came to putting Sailors's Wyoming achievements in perspective, longtime sports information director and athletic department administrator Kevin McKinney said, "He's considered one of our two or three all-timers. He was our first great player. A lot of people say he got us in the big time."

Once Sailors moved back to Laramie he became visible at many Cowboy athletic events. He attended all home football games, the men's and women's home basketball games, and for a time, through friendship with the coach, even went on the road to some women's basketball games.

Top left: The game ball from Wyoming's 1943 NCAA title win over Georgetown is on display in the school's trophy case in the Arena-Auditorium. (Photo by Lew Freedman.)

Top right: Kenny Sailors's University of Wyoming Athletic Hall of Fame plaque as it appears on the wall at the Arena-Auditorium in Laramie. (Photo by Lew Freedman.)

Kenny Sailors still attends University of Wyoming basketball games at the Arena-Auditorium on the Laramie campus. (Photo by Lew Freedman.)

He discovered that contrary to the Thomas Wolfe book and the oft-used phrase about being unable to go home again, he could very well return home to Laramie with very pleasing results.

"It was very fulfilling," said Sailors, who was also inducted into the Wyoming state Hall of Fame. "I got more attention than when I was here playing ball. All of a sudden. It was pretty good for me. It was really feeling like home. Not only the university treated me that way, but there were still people in the community who knew me. The younger brother of one of my old high school buddies remembered me. He saw me play. Wherever I go in town people know me. They think they know me even if they never saw me play."

At the start of the 2008–9 Wyoming basketball season, Sailors was honored in another very conspicuous way—his No. 4 jersey was retired and hung from the rafters at the Double A in a special ceremony. Kenny rated his own page in the team media guide with pictures of him as a player and gazing up at his jersey hanging near the ceiling. The write-up that accompanied the photos concluded with this paragraph: "Kenny Sailors, who now lives in Laramie and can be seen in the stands at most Wyoming games and practices, will forever be remembered by Cowboy fans as one of the greatest Cowboy players, and he will be remembered in the history of the game as one of the pioneers who made basketball the exciting game it is today."

About that jersey. Sailors received a replica for his own souvenir collection. But other replicas were produced and were selling for about $132, to the best of Sailors's knowledge.

"There's an outfit downtown that makes them and sells them," he said. "A lot of people bought them. I've signed probably four

Before the 2008–9 Wyoming basketball season Kenny Sailors's No. 4 jersey was retired and hung from the rafters at the Arena-Auditorium. (Photo courtesy the University of Wyoming.)

The cake for Kenny Sailors's ninetieth birthday featured a picture of the starting lineup of the 1942–43 Cowboys basketball team. (Photo courtesy the University of Wyoming.)

dozen of them. They've got my name and number on the back. It's a regular-sized shirt like I wore. They're still looking for my original one. I don't think it's around. I think Coach Shelton stopped giving it to people, but coaches change and athletic directors change and they forgot all about that."

Once Sailors's jersey was hung in the arena it was on view at all times, during games, practices, and on off-days. One day Sailors was in the building with a youngster who was the grandson of someone he knew and the retired jersey was pointed out to him. He looked at the human-sized Sailors and he looked at the oversized jersey on display like a piece of art and said, "Mr. Sailors, you were a lot bigger when you played."

Sailors got a grand chuckle out of that.

On January 14, 2011, the occasion of Sailors's ninetieth birthday, the university presented Sailors with a unique gift. It was actually a two-pronged present, one part perishable and one part durable. A special cake was baked that incorporated a photo of the starting five players on the 1942–43 team, Sailors, Volker, Milo Komenich, Jim Weir, and Lew Roney, immortalized as a group. Longer lasting, and now living in Sailors's residence, was a basketball inscribed, "Happy 90th Birthday to a Wyoming Treasure—Kenny Sailors, January 14, 2011." The basketball, Wyoming clothing, and various other basketball souvenirs decorate Sailors's home. He owns quite a few things that are brown and gold, or with the Cowboys' logo of a cowboy on a horse imprinted on them.

"In a small town like this, I see people I know everywhere I go," Sailors said.

That includes members of the university staff, who do indeed treat Sailors like a treasure. During a recent administration not a game passed when the then university president's wife didn't come over to greet Sailors and give him a hug. Once, he asked her what he should call the president and she said, "Kenny, don't call him president. He doesn't like that. Just call him Tom." At times Sailors was shaking hands with the university president and simultaneously hugging the school's first lady.

Frequently, Sailors attends games with his nephew Dale Sailors, son of his brother Bud, Erin, Dale's wife, and their children. People stop him for autographs but he keenly studies the play of the 2000s Cowboys. For a time Sailors even lived in a mother-in-law apartment with that younger generation of Sailorses, with his own entrance to their home on the outskirts of town. But being seven miles from the downtown action as his desire to drive and ability to do so diminished helped him decide to move back near the university, barely a jump shot away from the gym.

During a game between Wyoming and Texas Christian University (TCU), Sailors had some empty seats around him and a couple of old-time fans of the program sat in the row in front. A toddler was with them and Sailors periodically leaned forward and teased the child. A boy about age nine working as a bellboy, a friend of his nephew's son, came over to shake hands.

Coach Larry Shyatt has embraced Sailors's history and tries to keep him up to date with the program. Shyatt said that at the beginning of a season if Sailors is sitting in the stands at practice he will have his players go up into the seating area and shake hands. He also has Sailors address the team sometimes.

"He is a huge part of our history at Wyoming and I want to take advantage of that," Shyatt said. "Having him here does a lot for our team. He is a living example that winning the NCAAs is possible."

When Dan visits his father in Wyoming he can't get over how much attention is paid to him because of his basketball days. Dan was born after Sailors finished his college play, but he remembers some of his father's NBA time.

"I can still remember some of the old ballplayers," the younger Sailors said.

Demonstrating just how good his memory is, Dan Sailors cited Chuck Connors. Connors, later famous as *The Rifleman* on television, did play professional basketball with the Boston Celtics, as well as professional baseball.

When Dan walks around the streets of Laramie with his father, or attends an event with him, he marvels at how warmly he is treated, much like the treasure some refer to him as being.

"Treasure. That's a fair description," Dan Sailors said. "It's crazy when I go down and visit him. He's still kind of low-key and humble about it. I think it's kind of uncanny. I'm happy for him. It keeps him going."

Watching the Texas Christian game Sailors kept his eyes on Wyoming's top players and naturally enough he studied their form on jump shots. Sailors said he worked to get Adam Waddell, then a senior, to try a turnaround jumper. "He used it," Sailors said. Francisco Cruz, another senior, was from Mexico and Sailors thought he was the team's best player. (That year Wyoming won twenty games.) He exclaimed over the international flavor of the roster given that all of his teammates except Milo Komenich were from Wyoming. "We've had them from all over," Sailors said.

Occasionally, Sailors would riff about the changes between college basketball of the 1940s and the 2000s. Seeing about seven guys in suits sitting on the bench he couldn't get over how many assistant coaches a team employs these days. He also didn't put much stock in the doom-and-gloom outlook of not being able to win on the road because his Cowboys could always do it. They played thirty-three games in '42–43 and only nine were at home.

"The more they boo you the more they're afraid of you," Sailors said. "Just ignore them or laugh at them."

The crowd was not a big one for the Mountain West Conference game, but the spectators around Sailors were talking about how some of the roads along the highways in the state were closed because of blizzards even though Laramie was ducking the storm. Wyoming held off TCU for the win. The old Cowboy was satisfied. "Good ball game," Sailors said.

Over the last few years Sailors has fielded some requests from filmmakers who wish to create documentaries about his life, or do other interviews related to the NCAA championship history. Sailors's jump shot is not what it used to be and when a film crew from Texas urged him to take a shot, "They insisted that I shoot the basketball," Sailors said. "I bounced the ball into the basket. I said, 'Is that enough boys?'"

Sailors has slowed down a little bit. His hair is white, but he still has much of it. He wears glasses, but his vision isn't as sharp as it used to be. He needs hearing aids, but his memory is sharp. He still gets letters seeking autographs and although you won't find him typing on a computer, through a Laramie friend, Bill Schrage, he set up a website. Schrage has posted a wide variety of pictures and articles about Sailors on the site. Though Kenny is not computer savvy he has looked over the stuff. Most of it came from his scrapbook and most of that stuff is headed to the archives at the university as a permanent home.

In early March of 2012, the College Basketball Hall of Fame in Kansas City announced the members of its latest class. One of those selected was Kenny Sailors. It was the biggest honor of his life, the grandest recognition for his basketball accomplishments. It came as a surprise and Sailors accepted it as welcome news, but so many decades after he retired, and being past his ninetieth birthday, he was not gushing or jumping up and down about a ceremony scheduled seven months in the future.

"It is gratifying," Sailors said. "But at my age I could be gone in a day."

What was more immediate, though, was the NCAA flying Sailors, accompanied by Dale and Erin, to New Orleans, to be introduced at the 2012 Final Four as a new member of the Hall of Fame. That made the matter real in a hurry since it was only three weeks after the announcement.

"At halftime of the championship game they introduced us to seventy thousand people on the court," Sailors said. "That's the most I've ever seen in a building. I was worn out. I signed so many autographs. I was asked to pose for a lot of pictures. I don't know why they all wanted their pictures taken with an old man."

It took that type of journey, and appearing in front of a college basketball audience, for Sailors to realize that he was remembered beyond the boundaries of Wyoming and that fans who were not present at the creation of the jump shot or alive when he won that Most Valuable Player award in the NCAA tournament still knew who he was.

"All over the country people that have never seen me and don't know anything about me, or what I look like, they know about that jump shot," Sailors said. "I really don't know why everyone is so fascinated. Maybe they look at me as a living pioneer. That probably has a lot to do with it. They're starting to call me a legend."

Sailors smiled as he said that and laughed a bit. He was not comfortable with anyone thinking of him on such a grand scale. To him he was just a guy who played basketball, played it well, and did something a little bit different with his shot than the other players. He was proud of all that, but he thought being labeled a legend was a bit too much. However, he couldn't control that and although he shook his head, friends told him to accept the adulation gracefully. Kenny agreed that it was better to be remembered as a live legend than to be overlooked and forgotten and no longer breathing.

CHAPTER 18

A Hall of Famer

"WELCOME TO THE HALL OF FAME." The comment was made to Kenny Sailors, his relatives, and other inductees as they gathered in the lobby of the College Basketball Experience in downtown Kansas City prior to a VIP tour of the premises. It was a literal statement in two ways. Most of those collected in the building were going to be inducted into the Hall of Fame as members, and they were also about to embark on a walk around the Hall.

Sailors was accompanied by nephew Dale and his wife, Erin, and their ten-year-old son, Ethan, an avid basketball fan and a great appreciator of his uncle's career. A member of his local elementary school team, Ethan took full advantage of the interactive nature of the College Basketball Experience segment of the Hall of Fame, shooting hoops wherever it was allowed.

"I think he'll make a ballplayer," Sailors said of Ethan. As a boy, Ethan was still shooting two-handers, not jump shots yet, until his body grew into the shot, no doubt.

Everyone drank in the homages on display to the honorees, the various photographs and posters of those enshrined and the stories of the eras of basketball when they played. Other inductees and their friends and relations on the tour requested pictures with Sailors. He resisted entreaties and temptations to take any jump shots since he was then just shy of his ninety-second birthday. Someone teased Kenny by saying, "You should have put a patent on it." He joked that, "I've been practicing." But he really hadn't been. Certainly not with the gusto showed when he was an undergraduate at Wyoming.

Sailors, his family, and the other inductees and their families were the guests of honor at a luncheon, and the inductees were asked to autograph basketballs and photos for the Hall of Fame and others at the event. Sailors was being enshrined with former prominent college basketball figures such as Earl "The Pearl" Monroe, Willis Reed, Clyde Lovellette, Patrick Ewing, and Phil Ford, coaches Joe B. Hall and Dave Robbins and contributors Joe Dean and Jim Host.

The annual induction ceremony is conducted in conjunction with a college basketball tournament in late November, just before Thanksgiving, but at the front end of the season. In 2012 the event featured perennial national power Kansas, which was essentially the host team because of Lawrence, Kansas's proximity to Kansas City, Saint Louis University, Texas A&M, and Washington State. During the VIP reception and press conference with the honorees, coaches of some of those teams appeared to listen in, and some brought their players.

While most of the honorees were much younger than Sailors and played in an era when television was a major component in their careers, Lovellette and Sailors predated that time period. Dale Sailors, who is in his forties, never saw his uncle play for Wyoming or in the NBA, but had seen a video of Kenny's play.

"It's kind of an old film," Dale Sailors said. "It looks like it's playing tricks. He's [Kenny] just so much higher in the air than everybody else because he's taking the jump shot. When you're watching it, it's like they're standing still and he's not. It's unreal. It will surprise you."

During the luncheon, Ewing, who was one of Georgetown's greatest stars before his professional career with the New York Knickerbockers and his long career as an NBA assistant coach, stopped by Sailors's seat. The 7-foot-tall and powerfully built Ewing teased the older man as he towered over the seated Sailors because Wyoming's NCAA victory came at the expense of his Hoyas.

"I heard you were talking trash," Ewing joked. "I came to pick a fight because you kicked Georgetown's butt." The two men shook hands and smiled and exchanged congratulations over their acceptance into the Hall of Fame.

When officials set up the head table for the press conference, Monroe, known for his dazzling offensive moves and dribbling with the Knicks and the Baltimore Bullets, was seated next to Sailors and they chatted. Monroe was asked to ponder what basketball would be like without the jump shot that Sailors introduced.

"I guess we'd all be dunking," he said. "I can't imagine the game being played without the jump shot. So many things are done without us really knowing where they came from."

Sailors talked more about coaching in Angoon, Alaska, than taking his first jump shot. The crowd was spellbound as he explained about riding shotgun with those girls as they ran near the bear-infested dump. That was exactly the type of exotica most of them imagined going on in Alaska. When Sailors was welcomed he exaggerated his age slightly and said, "At ninety-two years of age, I'm glad to be anywhere."

Washington State Coach Ken Bone—who as the coach with Seattle Pacific University for many years made numerous trips to Alaska to play against the University of Alaska Anchorage and the University of Alaska Fairbanks—brought his entire squad to the event to hear Sailors and the other inductees talk about their time spent in the sport.

"I wanted to give them a glimpse of the history of basketball," Bone said. "I don't know if they'd heard of anybody here tonight except Earl Monroe before, but it's good for them to know about the history."

Also present was a solid contingent of Wyoming officials from sports information director Tim Harkins to former Coach Jim Brandenburg, who was proud of the Cowboys' involvement in the proceedings and Sailors's link to the program.

"We've got pictures that nobody else does of Kenny shooting the jump shot," Brandenburg said. "Kenny Sailors was the first person in the NBA to shoot it. It's been debunked, a couple of years ago, other claims. Kenny is the one who developed the mechanics of the jump shot. Hank Luisetti shot a one-hander. He took a step. Sportswriters in different parts of the country saw the running one-hander. They didn't have the expertise to sort them out [between Luisetti's and Sailors's styles]. This right here tonight puts the stamp on it that Kenny was the first."

The actual induction ceremony took place a couple of blocks away from the College Basketball Experience and Hall of Fame, but also in downtown Kansas City, at the Midland Theatre, a restored old-time showplace. The induction ceremony itself was filmed for a television show to be aired on ESPN.

One-by-one the inductees were called to the stage and individually presented with a gold medal hung around their necks. Then they sat in a chair and were asked questions by announcers Seth Davis, Pat Forde, and Jeremy Schaap.

"There is no greater honor than being inducted into your sport's Hall of Fame," Schaap said at the start of the seventh annual induction ceremony. "Every single one of them has changed the game in some way."

Brandenburg was dead right about the induction putting to rest any speculation or question about Kenny Sailors's connection to the jump shot. As part of the prerecorded introduction over the loudspeaker Sailors's name was tied to "the invention of the modern-day jump shot." Some seventy years after Sailors employed that jump shot to lead his Wyoming Cowboys to an NCAA title, it was a pleasing phrase to hear in public.

Although at times Sailors has said he can't remember if he made the first jump shot he ever took against Bud, on this occasion he told the audience, "The first one I shot, it went in." It's possible that it did and it's possible that given the passage of time since 1934 that Sailors doesn't always recall that detail.

Sailors recounted his youthful tale of playing basketball against his brother in Wyoming on the windswept plain, Bud's encouragement to develop the jump shot, and the time he put into it.

"It didn't come overnight," Sailors said. "I was jumping into people at first, not straight up in the air and I would get called for the offensive foul. I was getting called for the foul as much as I was making the shot. It took a year or two."

When the ceremony ended, Sailors had a large, round gold medal hanging around his neck. It was as if he had won an Olympic gold medal—and it probably felt as if he had. The first thing he said when talking to his family, though, was, "It's really heavy."

So was what it signified. After all of the honors collected so many years earlier, this was the frosting on the cake. The medal told Sailors he belonged, that he was now a member of an exclusive club—the College Basketball Hall of Fame. The front of the medal announced that with the words "National College Basketball Hall of Fame." The back of the medal read, "Kenny Sailors, 2012 Inductee."

Before the Sailorses left the building, however, the medal was on loan. Ethan got his first chance to wear it. Uncle Kenny took the weight off his shoulders, so to speak.

One night later, the Hall of Fame inductees were introduced to the thousands of basketball fans in attendance at halftime of a game at the Sprint Center. Sailors and his fellow enshrines waved to the fans and received a rousing ovation. The next day he was on an airplane back to Wyoming, back to Laramie, though the glow of the induction ceremony lingered for a little while.

The trip tired the aging Sailors, but he got a kick out of his moment in the spotlight, even though he was surprised that he and the others were being filmed for a TV show.

In November of 2012, at the age of ninety-one, Kenny Sailors was inducted into the College Basketball Hall of Fame during a ceremony in Kansas City when a gold medal signifying his selection was draped around his neck. (Photo by Lew Freedman.)

"I was happy," Sailors said. "I enjoyed myself. It was all interesting. I was surprised by all of the picture taking and the autographs. That medal is about the same thing they give in the Olympics. It was good for the university and good for the state. I feel good about it. I appreciate it. I really do."

The linking of his name with the jump shot as the "inventor of the modern jump shot," thrilled Sailors and in his mind added an entirely new level of acceptance to his feat.

"It'll give it more prestige now," Sailors said. "Some people thought it was a fad when I shot it. I could never believe that I was the first person who jumped in the air to shoot. Maybe someone back in the nineteenth century did. But I developed the jump shot they use today."

Sailors was in his nineties and he knew there would not be many more celebrations of his basketball days like this one, the moments that kept coming up so many decades after his greatest Wyoming achievements.

"It's kind of crazy," he said. "There are quite a few things I'm remembered for now. They still treat me pretty good around Laramie."

As it so happened, there was at least one more major go-around in store feting Sailors's basketball accomplishments from 1943 when the spring of 2013 rolled around. That year the NCAA Final Four was played in Atlanta and it was the seventh-fifth anniversary of the tournament's 1939 beginnings.

Quietly, well in advance of the championships, ESPN sent a film crew to Laramie to visit with the oldest living Most Valuable Player of the premier college basketball tournament in the land. Sailors had fun dealing with the visitors and word got around Laramie, of course. The general belief was that on the day of the Final Four semifinals ESPN was going to air a documentary about the history of the NCAA tournament and that Sailors would be part of it.

What everyone around Wyoming thought was that while their man Sailors was going to be highlighted in it the show would tell the same story they all knew. Surely the documentary would document Sailors's innovation of the jump shot, his All-American years at Wyoming, and winning that 1943 national championship.

But viewers who knew Sailors were in for a surprise. While the backdrop of the Sailors story was included, ESPN turned ninety-two-year-old Kenny Sailors into an actor for a day. The way the sports network told the story of NCAA history was by using Sailors as a narrator. Rather than filming Sailors at the University of Wyoming, in a gym, or at home, he was transplanted to a library.

Although the books themselves that he plucked from shelves were not real ones—they were labeled as NCAA playoffs by decade—Sailors, not a librarian, and not a famed announcer, played the role of narrator. One by one Sailors hauled out a book supposedly containing a decade's worth of college basketball history, opened it, and began talking about what happened.

For the first time at least since maybe a school play in elementary school, and maybe ever, Sailors was playing a part. All of the phone calls that flooded in to talk to him about it after the showing were from people who not only said they saw Sailors on the air, but that they were surprised to see what he was doing while he was on the air. The old cowboy certainly caught his public off-guard.

"It was fun," Sailors said when the plaudits rolled in following his fifteen-to-twenty-minute airing smack in the middle of the grandest college basketball week of the year. He got a laugh out of it and a laugh out of something else.

ESPN.com had an accompanying feature story on the history leading up to the seventy-fifth annual NCAA tournament and Sailors was included in that, too. In it Sailors was described as being "popular with the bingo-playing ladies at his senior living center" and having "the posture of the ex-Marine he is, a crew cut to match."

While Sailors may indulge in bingo, he does claim that he is the only resident of the center that still works out at all to try to stay in shape.

If Kenny Sailors originated the jump shot then the thousands and thousands of players that followed were imitating him. That was flattering, he admitted, but wasn't that copyright infringement, too?

"I should sue them, shouldn't I?" Sailors said with a twinkle in his eye. "Sue them for the use of my shot. Sue the players, every one of them that has been using my jump shot, but who hasn't contacted me and asked my permission."

When Sailors thinks back on his life he sees very little that he would have changed. He has nothing but warm feelings about Wyoming and his college days, even if he still can hardly believe how many people remember him and still contact him because of his All-American basketball play and for introducing the jump shot to college basketball and the NBA.

His marriage of nearly sixty years' duration to Bokie is something that is just as alive to him now as when they shared their days together.

"I miss Marilynne," Sailors said. "My whole life has pretty much been basketball and the outdoors. I loved Bokie, Wyoming, and Alaska—I had a lot of good years in Alaska—and I thank the Lord for my good fortune."

SOURCES

THE VAST MAJORITY OF QUOTES ATTRIBUTED to Kenny Sailors in this story about his life took place in face-to-face interviews with author Lew Freedman.

Lengthy interviews were recorded in Gakona, Alaska, during the summer months of 1993 and lengthy interviews were recorded in Laramie, Wyoming, in February of 2012.

In addition, over a period of several years the author conducted numerous telephone and face-to-face interviews with Kenny Sailors for additional material.

Since 1988, the author and Kenny Sailors have cooperated on articles about his life for numerous publications, including the *Anchorage Daily News*, *Alaska* magazine, *Basketball Times* magazine, and the 2012 NCAA Final Four program. Information obtained in the reporting of those articles was used in this manuscript.

The author was present at the 1990 Final Four dinner and games in the company of Kenny Sailors and at the events surrounding and including his induction into the College Basketball Hall of Fame in 2012.

In addition, the author and Kenny Sailors collaborated on a book entitled *Hunting the Wild Country* about Sailors's hunting experiences in Wyoming and Alaska that was published locally in Alaska in 1994.

Additional interviews were conducted by the author with:

Rick Anderson	Curt Gowdy	Bud Sailors
Johnny Bach	Michelle Howard	Dale Sailors
Ken Bone	Duane Klueh	Dan Sailors
Jim Brandenburg	Clyde Lovellette	Marilynne "Bokie"
Bobby Brown	Kevin McKinney	Sailors
Jack Cotton	Ray Meyer	Larry Shyatt
Bob Cousy	Earl Monroe	Denise Starr
Patrick Ewing	Bill Noonkesser	Floyd Volker
Ron Gleason	Jim Reese	

The University of Wyoming Sports Information Office has a large collection of old newspaper clippings from the 1940s era when Kenny Sailors played there. While the clippings are dated, they are not identified by newspaper individually, though the material was gathered from the *Laramie Boomarang*, the *Casper Star-Tribune*, the *Wyoming Eagle* in Cheyenne, and the *Denver Post*.

Publications that reported on Kenny Sailors that were cited in the manuscript are:

Casper Star-Tribune	NCAA.com	*Stanford Magazine*
Denver Post	*New York PM*	*The Sporting News*
ESPN.com	*New York Sun*	*Wyoming Eagle*
Laramie Boomerang	*New York Times*	
LIFE magazine	*Rocky Mountain News*	

SPORTS RECORD GUIDES
National Basketball Association Guide, 1972–73.
University of Wyoming men's basketball media guide, 2009–10.

WIRE SERVICES
Associated Press
United Press

BOOKS

Christgau, John. *The Origins of the Jump Shot: Eight Men Who Shook the World of Basketball*. Lincoln, NE: Bison Books, 1999.

Sailors, Kenny and Lew Freedman. *Hunting the Wild Country*. Anchorage, AK: Glacier Press, 1994.

Thorburn, Ryan. *Cowboy Up*. Fort Collins, CO: Burning Daylight, 2011.

Wolff, Alexander. *100 Years of Hoops*. New York: Oxmoor House, 1991.

Kenny Sailors
Basketball Honors

1934 Inventor of modern day jump shot.

1941–42 All-Skyline Conference selection.

1942–43 Captain of Wyoming Cowboys basketball team that finished 31–2.

1942–43 Most Valuable Player NCAA championships, leading Wyoming to title.

1942–43 All-Skyline Conference selection.

1943 Winner Chuck Taylor Award as best college player in United States.

1943 College All-American.

1943 Amateur Athletic Union All-American.

1945–46 All-Skyline Conference selection.

1945–46 College All-American.

1945–46 Winner Helms Foundation Award as best college player in United States.

1946–47 Member Cleveland Rebels, NBA.

1947–48 Member Chicago Stags/Philadelphia Warriors/Providence Steamrollers, NBA.

1948–49 Member Providence Steamrollers, NBA.

1949–50 Member Denver Nuggets, NBA.

1950–51 Member Boston Celtics/Baltimore Bullets NBA.

1993 Inducted as member of first class, University of Wyoming Intercollegiate Athletics Hall of Fame.

2005 Chosen as member of University of Wyoming All-Century Team.

2008 No. 4 playing jersey retired by University of Wyoming.

2012 Inducted into College Basketball Hall of Fame.

Kenny Sailors
Basketball
Statistics

COLLEGE

1940–41 University of Wyoming, 7.3 points per game.

1941–42 University of Wyoming, 9.4 points per game.

1942–43 University of Wyoming, 15.0 points per game.

1945–46 University of Wyoming, 7.8 points per game.

PROFESSIONAL/NBA

1946–47 Cleveland Rebels, 9.9 points, 2.3 assists per game.

1947–48 Chicago Stags/Philadelphia Warriors/Providence Steamrollers, 11.9 points, 1.3 assists per game.

1948–49 Providence Steamrollers, 15.8 points, 3.7 assists per game.

1949–50 Denver Nuggets, 17.3 points, 4.0 assists per game.

1950–51 Boston Celtics/Baltimore Bullets, 8.2 points, 2.5 assists per game.

Career averages 12.6 points, 2.8 assists per game.

Author Lew Freedman (left) and Kenny Sailors on the campus of the University of Wyoming in November of 2013. Photo by Bill Schrage.

About the Author

LEW FREEDMAN IS THE AUTHOR of more than seventy books about Alaska and sports and he is one of the most decorated sportswriters in the history of the United States Basketball Writers Association for his coverage of college basketball.

Freedman is the former sports editor of the *Anchorage Daily News*—in which capacity he got to know Kenny Sailors and his family—and has written about college basketball for such publications as the *Philadelphia Inquirer*, *Chicago Tribune*, and *Basketball Times* magazine. He is currently sports editor of the *Casper Star-Tribune* in Wyoming.

CPSIA information can be obtained at www.ICGtesting.com
Printed in the USA
BVOW11s1605300114

343462BV00003B/4/P